The Monkey Mountain Story

A new way to learn and do Tai Chi

Michael White

*To Johanne
My fellow sometime tenor.
I hope we get to sing again — and maybe
follow up with Tai Chi
Michael
May 2013*

AuthorHouse™
1663 Liberty Drive
Bloomington, IN 47403
www.authorhouse.com
Phone: 1-800-839-8640

© 2013 Michael N. D. White. All Rights Reserved.

No part of this book may be reproduced, stored in a retrieval system, or transmitted by any means without the written permission of the author.

Published by AuthorHouse 03/13/2013

ISBN: 978-1-4817-1607-9 (sc)
         978-1-4817-1608-6 (e)

Library of Congress Control Number: 2013902704

This book is printed on acid-free paper.

The views expressed in this work are solely those of the author and do not necessarily reflect the views of the publisher, and the publisher hereby disclaims any responsibility for them.

Dedication

I would like to dedicate this book to the teachers who gave me Tai Chi, Master Moy Lin Shin, Dr. Zhu Gwang Ya and Dr. Peter Kun Yang, and to Norma and Al Levitt and all my friends of the South Riverdale Seniors Wellness Group, and to Elsie Petch who has been with this from the beginning.

Contents

Part I	7	The Song of the Trip to Monkey Mountain
Part II	10	The Manual for Monkey Mountain Tai Chi
Chapter 1	10	The Tai Chi trip up to Monkey Mountain Lookout
Chapter 2	24	Going Down the Mountain
Chapter 3	45	A Short Preface about Tai Chi, the Trip up Monkey Mountain and Monkey Mountain Story Tai Chi
Chapter 4	51	The 27 Tai Chi Moves of the Monkey Mountain Story
Chapter 5	79	The Animals in the Monkey Mountain Story
Annex 1	81	The 15 Monkey Mountain Stations
Annex 2	83	The 24 Moves of the Yang Short Form Tai Chi ; Dr. Peter Yang's Traditional set; The Monkey Mountain Story Warmup Set ; The Five Chee Kung Animals
Annex 3	90	Where is Monkey Mountain?
Annex 4	90	References

The Monkey Mountain Story: A New Way to do Tai Chi

Introduction

This book is about a new and different way to do Tai Chi.

Monkey Mountain Tai Chi weaves Tai Chi into a story of a journey up an imaginary Mountain somewhere in western China. This story was developed to help people learn Tai Chi. The story gives the leader of a group a series of pictures which allow people of all ages to follow and enjoy the 24 movements that make up a Tai Chi set, with the series of moves from Dr. Peter Yang's short traditional set.

The Tai Chi in the Monkey Mountain story is based on the traditional 24 move short Yang Style Tai Chi. This is the most popular Tai Chi in China and the world over today.

Tai Chi is a dance. Each time it is played, 24 – 26 moves are done. This is called a Tai Chi set. A set can take from 5 to 20 minutes to play. Each trip up Monkey Mountain is a Tai Chi set. The story takes the players through 15 different stations in the trip up the mountain and the return home.

The Monkey Mountain story started in a Canadian community health centre. Over the past ten years, it has been successfully introduced to groups attending community health and recreational centres and in retirement and nursing homes, in diabetes and mental health programs. Presentations at community college activation programs and at the Toronto Island Sunshine Center have resulted in Monkey Mountain being taken to many settings.

Tai Chi has real benefits for all ages. But especially as we get older, we can lose the ability or confidence to walk and move about easily. That loss can be the result of physical changes or simply because of life factors such as our constant use of chairs. Consider falls alone. A serious fall in later years is often the event that may begin the loss of independence.

People who do Tai Chi and who do the Monkey Mountain story really do improve their balance and flexibility. They avoid or recover from near falls. They gain or regain their ability to walk or to enjoy exercise. Being able to move about with confidence encourages socialization and adds to the enjoyment of living. There is also a calming logic to the moves of Tai Chi and the Monkey Mountain story. The concentration required to learn and play the moves clears the mind and relieves stress. Tai Chi is sometimes called a moving meditation.

Tai Chi is normally learned over a few months. The Monkey Mountain story opens the world of Tai Chi to those frustrated or unable to follow the standard approach to learning because of memory issues or the fear of failure. The story can also be done seated. Some who learn the story will encouraged to go on to learn the Tai Chi set and lead others in the story and in Tai Chi.

    Storytelling is also a proven powerful way of communication. The joy of a familiar story takes one on a journey of imagination alone or with a group. The visual images, the detailed drawing of the mountain journey, and even the toy animals that have become part of the Monkey Mountain story, give Tai Chi cues at the 15 stations along the way. Music also plays an integral part of the experience.

    It is now time to take this story and its Tai Chi to others. The story and its Tai Chi gives caregivers who work to care for seniors or even just people who care for their neighbours, a new, gentle, effective and safe tool for their wellbeing as a daily or weekly exercise. When more and more of our population is aging and more and more can enjoy and benefit from it, it is time for the Monkey Mountain story, a new way to teach or lead them to do this gentle but proven good exercise, Tai Chi.

    The Monkey Mountain Tai Chi story helps the players, the teachers, and the leaders to be playful and patient. Come and join us.

Part I

The Song of the Trip to Monkey Mountain
The Song of the Trip to Monkey Mountain.
Read and Play to the Tai Chi Music

    Have some tea and a light breakfast. Rise with the sun early in the morning, in the valley under the mountains. Our cottage is beside a great river. Sounds of the village are around us. In our garden we greet the sun, warm on our faces, that rises over the mountains to the east.
    We are going on a trip up to the Monkey Mountain Lookout today.

    Our little ponies wait at the gate of the garden. Lift their saddles from the rack and throw them on their shoulderss. Cinch them under fat bellies and attach bridles. Throw a leg over their backs. Ride down across the fields toward the mountains.

    A small stream flows under the bridge, down from the hills above. We dismount and watch. Great white cranes dance in the wet fields beside the marshes on the river edge. How many ages have these lovely birds returned to dance in these mountain valley marshes and fields.

We climb the ridge to the Lookout.
Leave our ponies to the children to take home. Open the farmer's gate. Wave as we pass the workers in the fields. Wave to those in rice paddies above. Follow the paths to where the hillside's forest and the bamboo thickets begin.

The second gate opens to the path threading the way up through the trees where the birds are singing and squirrels scuffle.

Walk up the steep path to the top of the ridge. There are characters written on the arch by the Lookout. "Beware of the Monkeys".

The view is lovely to the north and east from the Lookout.
It is peaceful far below in the villages along the banks of the river and the boats on the water. Behind us is the rock with the poem of the young lovers carved on it that Gwang Ya told us about.

But where are the monkeys?

Soon enough, the first small monkey band arrives.
They beg for food, now all about us, young and old, agile little people. We back away.

Above us a bell rings. The old man of the mountain and his bell. There is food for the monkey band up by his cottage. They leave us. We can relax and enjoy the Lookout.

We will thank the old man with some gifts and food the next time we come up. Or give some to the young people from the valley who go up where he teaches them about the way of life and monkeys.

Too soon, it is time to go down the ridge from the Lookout.
We use the back trail.

In a valley beside us we see small birds struggling in the hunters' nets.
We stop and carefully free them. We think about lowering the nets.

These may have been the bright little birds whose songs we heard as we climbed to the Lookout. Hold them gently when you have disentangled them. Release them away from that net you almost cannot see.

Above us a great eagle soars. We spread our arms like her wings. She swoops down over the mists on the lake.

Our hands float like clouds.

Sweep down, like the wind lifting the waves on the water.

Sweep across, carrying the clouds over the valleys and the peaks.

A raven flies to the roof of the temple.
Beside the road below us, round gates open into the temple courtyard.

Monks, yellow robes, young and old, are doing their exercises. We could copy their leaps and rolls and strikes. They kick to the right and the left. Their play keeps their bodies supple and their minds bright.

After, there will be time for calm chanted prayers, meditation, music and work. We take an offered drink and continue down our road.

The round gates close.

There are snakes warming themselves on the road down the mountainside. Are you brave and agile enough to sweep them off the road? Can you lift your foot high like a rooster to avoid their strikes? Walk carefully around them and pick berries from the roadside bushes.

Below us we can hear singing and laughter in the village.
We turn the corner at the bottom of the road. We are in the village square. All around us are weaving looms. Brightly dressed ladies of the village work at the looms, throwing shuttles of colored cotton, linen and silk back and forth. This is where the singing and laughing came from.
Men who are not in the fields sit in the sun. Small children play.
Learn to throw shuttles if you can. Choose some bright cloth to take home. A bell rings, tea is brought, work stops but not the laughter.

At the dock beside the square there is a fisherman we know. He will take us across the river back to our village. Wave goodbye to the weavers.
A single oar moves the boat into the current. We will need the sails. Our village is upstream. But first we pick up fishing poles and throw the lines out into the river.
How big is the bright silver carp on the floorboards. Spread your arms like opening a fan to show what you have caught. Help the fisherman raise the sails of the boat. The mountains are reflected in the water of the wide river.

There is a big bed of lotusses beside our village dock. The great green leaves float on the water. They gather sunlight. Their stems take it down to the roots in the river mud. Green flowerlets spear up from the bottom. They pierce the surface and burst open into beautiful new lotus blooms.
A small dragonfly lifts off the lotus petal, skims away across the river. An island over there has a dark cave.

The Island holds the legend of the dragon and the phoenix. The dragon gathers all the power of the sun that shines on this valley river and lake among the mountains. It roars and shakes its scaly head and spiny tail. They call him Yang.
And from time to time the phoenix, who is made from all the power that comes from the earth and the waters, flies to the island from far up the valley. Her beautiful tail, if you see her, has all the colors of the flowers, the iridescence of birds and the sparkle of fish. They call her Ying.
One can almost hear and see them through the haze over the river on a day like this says the fisherman.

The boat docks. Our journey is almost over. The woodsman sells sweet pine logs to be chopped into kindling for our kitchen fire. And cut another log block for the next person.
We gather up our fish, our wood, the blanket from the village of the weavers. Climb the hill to the cottage. Feed the chickens and the ponies.

We have finished our trip to the Lookout and Monkey Mountain.
Now is time to be home and enjoy our friends. That is the way to live the old man told us. The sun is setting behind the mountains. The valley is quiet.

Part 2

The Manual for Monkey Mountain Tai Chi

Chapter 1

The Tai Chi trip up to Monkey Mountain Lookout

I am going to have you join me on a trip up to the so-called Monkey Mountain Lookout. Monkey Mountain is the name of a small ridge in Western China. It is also the name to the popular lookout on top of the ridge. The ridge and the lookout are very similar to the Mount Douglas lookout on the top of that small mountain in the south of Vancouver Island, British Columbia in the west of Canada. The difference is the monkeys.

The monkeys have lived on Monkey Mountain ever since the lookout was built. They were there long before the old man built his little house and shrine further up the ridge. Young and older people from the valley come up and visit him. The old man came and looked after the monkeys. He learned to live with them and enjoy them. He is a very patient old man.

Monkey Mountain is an imaginary mountain. Maybe it exists somewhere in far western China in the foothills of the Himalayas. There it would be complete with its lookout, its monkeys and its old man. The slopes, paths, valleys, its old roads, its temple and the villages around it, even the great river and the dragon island and its cave are all part of the Monkey Mountain story landscape.

Join me climbing this mountain. It is the new way to experience a wonderful exercise that was invented a long time ago in China. This climb is the new way to experience and learn Tai Chi.

We begin our outing from the back door of a little cottage. It is on the edge of a little village in the valley below Monkey Mountain. The village is beside the broad river that flows south through the mountains. The cottage is on the small main road through the village. Its back door overlooks a walled garden full of flowers and vegetables and chickens. Beyond the garden, outside a gate, fields and more gardens run down to the riverbanks.

Beyond these fields, a small stream flows into the river. A beautiful old stone bridge leads over the stream. The road runs along the shore. Farm gardens, fields and rice paddies rise up on the lower slopes of the hillside. Above the rice paddies are woods and bamboo thickets. These go up the side of Monkey Mountain ridge.

Up there on the ridge, a long time ago they built a path up the ridge and a lookout. From there you can see the great foothills and mountains that stretch into the distance.

The sun rises and we start our trip up to the Monkey Mountain lookout. The early rays of the morning sun shine on the back steps of the cottage, and on the garden, the flowers and vegetables.

"The sun rises" is also the name of the first movement of Tai Chi. It is the traditional first move of all the different kinds of Tai Chi that have been done all over China for a thousand and more years, since and before this exercise was first given this name.

To greet the sun, we raise our arms. It is as if the sun were on our finger tips. Our arms rise with the calm slowness that you will learn is special to Tai Chi. The movement could even be as slow as the rising of the sun itself if this were possible. For most of us it is just slow and smooth. The slowness of "the sun rises" will be the careful way of all the 23 and more Tai Chi moves that will follow as we climb the mountain and back.

The sun shines down on the cottage, the garden and flowers and the chickens. Your shoulders relax and your arms come down in front of you. Pick up your pack with some food and water. We begin our trip.

Ride ponies to the base of Monkey Mountain. "Comb the wild horses' manes" in Tai Chi

In the field beyond the garden gate, small mountain ponies are grazing. At the gate, we can reach over to the rack to pick up saddles and bridles. An apple slice will bring the ponies over. We are going to ride them over to the base of Monkey Mountain.

Grasp a saddle firmly. It's heavy, made of wood and leather in the country mode with bright ribbons, brass buttons, padding and stirrups of wood and leather. Throw it over the pony's back. Tie it tightly beneath the animal's stomach. Put on the bridle. If your imagination is good, swing a leg up over the pony's back and mount up.

We will ride the Ponies over to the Mountain but in the second movement of our Tai Chi set. It is called **"Comb the wild pony's mane"**.

To ride your pony and comb its mane, step forward, raise your hand, palm up, fingers relaxed, and "comb" the hair of the your pony's thick mane. Step forward with the other foot and comb with the fingers and palm of the other hand. Right foot forward, right hand combs. Left foot, left hand combs. Repeat, left, right, left, right, left. This is how we will ride our ponies through the gate, down the trail across the fields towards the river and the mountains beyond, in Tai Chi style.

When we ride our ponies we will also learn a special Tai Chi way of walking. It is among the most important lessons of Tai Chi. It is how you use Tai Chi to strengthen your legs and improve your balance. It is different from the ordinary walking we use in our day to day ordinary lives. Later we will also use the way of walking in other moves of Tai Chi, and it will affect and improve how you walk or even streide in your day to day business.

At first, learning Tai Chi walking will be slow, even difficult. We practice it as we take our ponies across the fields. But we get better and stronger. We learn to transfer all our weight from one foot to the other. Each step is done with care because it tests our balance. Someone described this Tai Chi way of walking as how you would need to walk across a rough floored forest safely on a very dark moonless night.

We ride the ponies with our new careful way of walking, one step after another, combing the pony's mane each step, across the fields toward Monkey Mountain, slow at first, then more smoothly. Your legs become more used to the movements, your balance steadies. You will begin to become graceful.

There is more to tell you about "Combing the Ponies' manes".

In Tai Chi, as we comb our pony's mane, the raised and sweeping palms of our hands are defensive moves. "Combing the wild horses' manes" is part of Tai Chi's other job. It is a defensive martial art. We clear the way ahead of us, parting the way with our hands as we ride.

We ride across the fields, down the slope toward the river. A few steps of the Tai Chi walking and combing are enough to take you across the fields, down to the river's edge and up onto a small bridge.

We have arrived at the banks of the great river. The old stone bridge spans the fast rivulet that flows down from the hills above. Here, we leave our ponies with a young girl of the village. She will ride them back to their home fields.

We step up onto the bridge. Now we see a sight that has enthralled the people of China since before history.

In the marshes and wet lands beyond the bridge and beside the big river, tall white cranes are feeding, courting and sparring.

"The White Cranes Cool Their Wings" is how in China they describe the dances of the big white birds. These dances are sometimes stately, sometimes humorous. Our Tai Chi will mimic the white cranes cooling their wings in the next moves that we learn on our trip up the Mountain.

In North America we are more familiar with great blue herons of our rivers and marshes. They do mating dances on their great nests. But these are nothing compared to the dancing of the cranes. In Canada there are Sandhill Cranes. They also dance. Some Cranes are rare. The big white Whooping Cranes of western Canada have almost gone altogether.

The most famous cranes of China are tall and white, with flashes of red on their heads. Cranes do their wonderful dances all over the world,. They leap, raise and lower their wings and heads. They greet, they court and dance in crany rivalries in the fields and wetlands beside the great river and lakes.

All over China and in America from times before man can remember, and in the north of Europe and Russia, the cranes returned each spring from their long winter migrations to Japan, or in America, to the Caribbean or other warm lands south. They arrive in the fields and marshes, often fearless among the men and women working there. They make nests, laid their eggs and raised their tall young crane "colts" in the fields and marshes along the rivers and lakes all over the world, In China they are the subjects of paintings and poems. They are the symbols of life to the Chinese since before history.

From the bridge we watch them. We copy their dance in the Tai Chi movements of "White Cranes Cool their Wings"

Step up on the toe of your foot. Spread your hands like feathers on each arm that become your wings. Raise one hand high, one wing up, your other hand down, the other wing down,. One hand up, the other down. Stretch tall and strong like the male cranes, or beautifully, elegantly and softly like the females.

But we have a mountain to climb. We turn away from the river towards the Mountain.

We cross the bridge and pass on. We will do our careful Tai Chi walking toward the mountains.

We open a farmer's gate. Follow the paths up to Monkey Mountain. They run across the fields by the river, then upward among the gardens and along paths over the rice paddies built on the lower slopes of the Monkey Mountain ridge.

Monkey Mountain is not a very big mountain. In fact, it is just a ridge of the bigger mountains behind. But for our story, and for the people who live nearby, with its Lookout and its monkeys, it is a special mountain.

Now, for us, it will take three Tai Chi "steps" to climb Monkey Mountain.

In our trip up the Mountain side, we will also learn to do the Tai Chi move called **"Carry a tiger up the mountain"**.

A small tiger club has become lost down the mountain in the village. As we walk up the paths toward the Mountain we will carry the young animal back up the mountain to his calling mother. On another day there was a baby panda bear who had wandered down along the rice paddy paths and got hopelessly lost away from the bamboo thickets. Carrying them back up to the woods becomes part of our Tai Chi.

Past the bridge, we open and pass through a farmer's gate. With our little animals, we will Tai Chi walk into the lower fields and gardens. Then we will follow up along the paths through the rice paddies to where another gate keeps the animals out from the forest above. Our climbing will be slow, careful, doing our Tai Chi walking.

Carrying the cubs with us makes the job of climbing the mountain a little harder. With each Tai Chi step, we change the cubs from one side to the other. This turning is part of Tai Chi's work on our bodies. It ensures that for each step we firmly, balance and turn our hips and our weight from one leg to the other. We do this each time, for each of the three steps we will take up the Mountain. It adds to our work but improves our balance and strengthens our legs as we walk and climb.

The Woods

Above the top paddies, we open the next gate. Now we climb with our cubs along the footpath that threads its way up among the trees on the upper forest slopes of Monkey Mountain. This is our second "step" up the mountain side. This is the realm of cool woods, bamboo thickets, small streams, birds and small animals. A woodpecker knocks, frogs call, birds sing, squirrels and rabbits rustle.

Above the trees, we arrive at the bottom of the steep stone track and rough steps up the mountainside. This will be the third step up the Monkey Mountain ridge to the Lookout. Brush twigs and stones off the path with one hand. With the other, carry your tiger or panda cub up this steep path as carefully and gently as you did the previous two steps.

Above, at last, we reach and open the final gate, this time with a carved sign telling us that we have arrived at the famous, ancient Mountain Lookout of the Monkeys and warning us of the monkeys.

Let the tiger cub go. Let the panda scamper off. Their mothers are waiting in the woods. Walk over to the stone wall. Now you can look out at the wonderful views on the other side of Monkey Mountain ridge.

Step up on the Monkey Mountain Lookout.

This Monkey Mountain Lookout we walk out onto is a fine lookout. Long ago the floor was levelled and lined with flat rocks. There were stone benches built to relax on. A strong wall overlooks the steep drop to the valley on the other side. The Lookout faces north to the snow capped peaks. To the east, you look down to the river with its villages and river traffic. Behind us, the ridge rises up and there is a small building with a courtyard and a bell.

The view from the Monkey Mountain Lookout is famous. Some are inspired to play music, some to paint, some to write poetry. Young lovers come up here to celebrate their love. It is the magical sight of the hills, the great distant snow and glacier covered mountains to the west and north. the valleys below, the rice paddies, the woods, the wide lake, the river below, the fishermen's boats, the villages, the sights the sounds far off.

Zhu Gwang Ya, my young friend who taught me the 24 move Yang Style Tai Chi came from south China on a visit to Canada. He was a professor of Chinese Architecture at South China University in Nanjing. He came in 1990 and gave a lecture on traditional Chinese gardens at the University of Guelph School of Landscape Architecture.

He told us about a wall in a garden on a mountain like this, near his home in southeast China. There, long ago, a young lover painted a poem of undying love to his maiden on a rock by a lookout above the valley. The young man went away to the imperial capital to serve China far off to the east. The lovers would never meet again. The poem was carved on the wall and the poem and the wall became famous.

Before he came to visit Canada, Gwang Ya worked on that garden to rebuild the wall where the young lover's poem had later been carved on a wall, long ago. The garden had fallen into disuse and the wall had begun to fall down. He redesigned the area and the wall was rebuilt. Gwang Ya went back to his family and his university in Nanjing in southern China a year later. We also have not heard from each other since.

Step Up and Play the Fiddle

Here on the lookout, we can relax, sit and take our violin or flute from our packs. Let our imaginations make the tunes.

The Tai Chi move done here on the top of the mountain is called "Step Up and Play the Fiddle". We step forward. Then step up with the other foot, and sit back comfortably on that back leg. Or just sit back on one of the benches. Our hands rise up in front of us. It is the way of holding and playing our imaginary violin or flute. It is also a firm defensive move.

We can make tea and take out our sandwiches or steamed buns. But take care before we eat, or when we rustle of papers. We are about to find out why this place lives up to its name, the Lookout of the Mountain of the Monkeys.

We are also about to need the next moves in the Tai Chi set.

Step back to repulse the monkeys

Like a lot of famous mountains of China, this mountain ridge has its band of monkeys. They are the Children of the Monkey King. They are the children of Hanuman in India. These mountain monkeys are brash. Their eyes are sparkling. They are intense, insistent, and always hungry. The whole band, the tough old leader, the senior ladies, the young males, the mothers with their babies on their backs and their older children around them, they all come to the Lookout. Dancing down among the trees and rocks, from above on the ridge.

It is useful now that in earlier warmup exercises we learned "Step Back and Repulse the Monkeys". It was practice in how to discourage mountain monkeys. You now will need to step back and repulse these monkeys. Do it carefully. Step back, push forward. Then look behind you before you step back again.

The younger monkeys are playful and delightful. The older ones are more serious and intense. This is why we have learned to play "Step back to repulse the monkeys". We push forward with one hand and step back. Push with the other hand, step back. But remember, look behind where you are stepping. There may be another mischievous animal behind you. Push carefully but firmly, step by step back. That is the only way to keep monkeys at bay.

The monkeys will pry into your pack, into your pockets. They will try to climb up on your shoulders. They will reach small hands into your hair. We hold onto your things and hold our tempers as best we can. Some of us will share our lunch with the gentler ones.

But then, from higher up the ridge, a bell rings.

The Hermit of Monkey Mountain Ridge's Bell

As quickly as they arrived, the monkey band gathers up the babies and all scamper back up the mountain. Somewhere up there, the old Taoist hermit of the mountain top has put out food for his monkeys. This is food brought up to him from the villages around by his students. They bring more than enough for the hermit and for their own lunches while they visit for their classes. They have also been told to bring enough good things for their teacher's monkey band. His monkey helper rings the dinner bell. The rest of the monkey band knows that bell means food for them all. As quickly as they came, old and young, the monkeys leave us to the quiet at the Lookout. All Chinese mountains need a good old hermit.

Once again we can relax and enjoy the beauty of the views from the Lookout. Below and beside us are the green foothills. Far beyond that are clouds and the blue and white peaks in the distance. The sun shines, the air is cool and clear. Below is the river. On it, there are boats, and along the banks are the many villages.

Soon enough, it is time to pack up our lunches before the monkeys comeback and leave the lookout to begin our trip home. A steep rough paved road leads down the other side of the ridge through the trees.

We begin another part of our trip.

Chapter 2

Going Down the Mountain

"Freeing the Tangled Songbirds" or Tai Chi's "Grasping the Bird's Tail"

    In a side valley beside the road, villagers from below have hung nets to catch birds for eating. But now the nets are unattended. In them, small brightly colored songbirds have become entangled and are struggling.

We stop to disentangle, and free the song birds from the hunters' nets. We carefully take the net strands from the wings, body and claws of the small birds. Freed, but we gently hold them for a moment. Then, away from the net, we release each to fly off into the woods around us. Then if I were you, I would lower the nets.

Reaching out and freeing the songbirds, we will be doing moves that are based on the Tai Chi moves called **"Grasping the Bird's Tail"** changed for the Monkey Mountain story.

The Yang style Tai Chi's moves called "Grasping the Bird's Tail" have four parts. Each part is important because together they are the moves used in the famous play-fighting, sparring game of Tai Ch called "Push Hands".

Push Hands is played with two people facing each other, Each player places their feet firmly, steps forward and entwines their hands with their opponents'. Then each player pushes forward, or leans back to take the push without falling. The game of Push Hands is played to test each player's stability and Tai Chi. It is a serious game that helps improve understanding of how Tai Chi works for balance, stability and resilience, and not necessarily just strength.

In the first move of "Grasp the bird's tail" and in Push Hands we stand facing an opponent or player. We reach forward with the back of one hand to touch and if necessary ward off a blow or push. This move is called Peng, in Chinese, "warding-off" or turning aside, in English.

Next, if the push is strong, reach forward with both hands. Grasp the opponent's arm and pull the opponent toward you and to the side past you. This is the "grasped bird's tail", the "pull down" or Lu, in Chinese, the second part of "grasping the bird's tail". If your opponent is not aware, he or she will be pulled off balance, and you win that time.

But if the opponent recovers, you will need more. Cross your hands, and firmly block ahead of you with your crossed hands. This is the powerful Chi, "block", part of Push Hands. Stalemate.

So, next, pull your hands apart, lean back, and pull down with both hands.

Finally push out sharply with both hands. These are the moves called An, meaning "separate and push".

Tai Chi Push hands is played as rapid series of moves. It teaches self defense through play. Push Hands is learning fun with friends It can be much stronger with more serious opponents.

Grasping Birds' Tails becomes Freeing the Song Birds.

In our trip up and down Monkey Mountain we have changed the form and spirit of "Grasping the Bird's Tail" to "Freeing the Songbirds". On our trip we are doing moves for exercise and enjoyment. We add saving some songbirds. The moves are very much the same for your legs, waiste and back. Free, the songbirds fly off up into the woods and trees.

Far above us we see a mountain eagle soaring in the wind.

This is Tai Chi. We now become the eagle.

``Become an Eagle``. Fly Like the eagle. Wave your hands like clouds

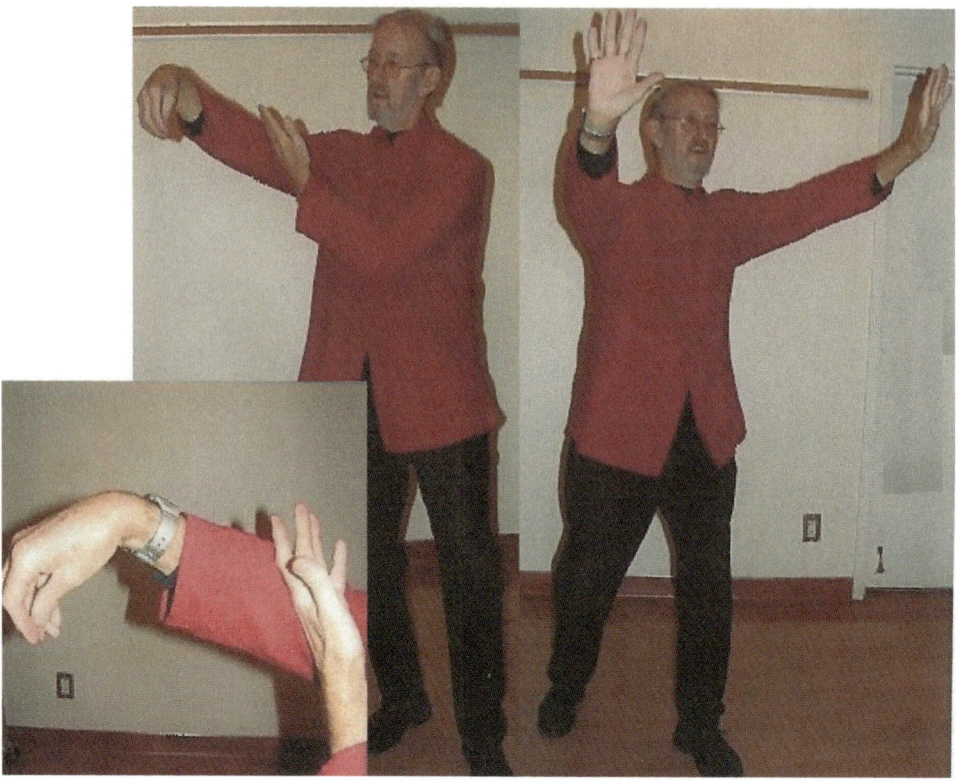

Lift one hand. Turn it down to form the head and beak of the eagle. Fit your other hand into the crook of the elbow as your folded wing. The picture gives an idea, but have your leader or teacher show you how to become an eagle.

In our story we become and then fly like the eagle. We spread our arms as the wings of and float on the winds high up in the sky. This movement increases the bloodflow to your heart.

The eagle swoops down from the blue through the mists over the lake below and soars back up into the clouds. First one hand swoops down like the eagle through the mists above the river and back up into the sky.

Then the other hand swoops down and up. We alternate our hands. We are here learning to do the beautiful, powerful Tai Chi move called
" Wave Hands Like Clouds". When we repeat these moves, we also can move our feet, stepping out and then back in together, as our weight changes from one side to the other as our arms swoop.

Our moving hands change. First they are the wingtips of an eagle. Then they sweep back and forth as lightly as floating clouds. Or they move like the wind blowing and sweeping the clouds across the mountain skies or across the waves on the river below.

I recall on a summer's day on an island by a lake in Canada, a wonderful older lady doing and enjoying these moves. Her hands really floated like clouds in front of her face.

In Yang Tai Chi, to start "Wave Hands Like Clouds", you throw out one arm to the side and curve your hand to make the head and beak of the eagle. When this move is done fast, it becomes the aggressive Tai Chi martial art movement called " Snapping the Whip" or "Single Whip".

The aggressive "Single Whip" image and move is gently changed in the Monkey Mountain story. Instead your more gently curved hand becomes the head and beak of the eagle. Your arm, folded in the crook of your elbow, opens out like the eagle's wing. The each arm sweeps down across the surface of the lake and up to float like clouds or the wind across the valley.

The eagle above us flies down the side of the mountain. It alights in a pine tree beside the walls of a large temple building. A raven flies over to the roof of a temple on the side of the hill. As we approach, the great round doors of the temple courtyard open. We are welcomed in to watch and join the Shaolin Buddhist monks who are practicing their exercises.

Play Kung Fu with the Monks of the Shaolin Temple

The exercises of the Buddhist monks in their temples includes play fighting, aggressive and defensive moves that have become known as Kung Fu. Much of the strength, balance and energy of their Shaolin exercises and skill is like that of the Taoist inspired Tai Chi. Buddhist and Taoists have shared the benefits of their martial arts and exercises, for most of their long histories in China.

The monks leap, kick and strike in the air. They strengthen their bodies, their minds and their spirits. Their exercises turn anger and violence into defensive play.

Their activities are called "Kung Fu", the name given to their training. The sets of exercises they do are "Kung", Chinese for work. What they try to achieve is "Fu", which is skill from all their learning and practice.

Like Tai Chi, Kung Fu exercises develop strength, good health and good balance. Also, these arts help to give calmness and self confidence that come from knowing self protection. The monks are preparing for long, good lives. They work, play their Kung Fu, study or learn by sitting quietly, chanting and meditating. Like Tai Chi, these are the ways to care for yourself and others in your trip through life. This is what we are doing in our trip up and down Monkey Mountain.

Tai Chi is sometimes called "Moving Meditation". It is also called a martial art. Tai Chi is also sometimes called Kung Fu, "skill, work done well". It is the gentle Kung Fu. It is a gentle martial art.

Tai Chi was the play of monks and people who studied the ancient "Way of Life", whether it was the Tao of the poems of Lao Tzu or the teachings of the Buddha . The Tao, or the Way, was what the poet Lao Zu wrote about in his volumes of poetry called the "Tao Te Ching", the classic Chinese book of poems, "Tao", the Way, and "Te", poems about how to live the Way. Old Lao was writing more than 2,500 years ago.

There are differences for the students of Taoism and those of Buddhism in their approaches to the mysteries of life. But the two great Chinese religions, along with the teaching of the philosopher Confucius, exist together in China, mostly in harmony, with "one heart towards heaven". They have their places in modern China as well. My first teacher believed that the way should be helpful for all peoples.

We watch and copy the monks' kicks. The toe or heel strikes test their strength and balance.

Cross your hands in front of you. Lift your hands up, then lift one knee. Straighten your leg. This is a kick in Kung Fu or Tai Chi. Watch and copy your chosen leader or teacher.

Step forward and repeat, lifting the other knee and kicking. Repeat again with your toe up as a kick with the heel. Or kick with the toes down as a sweeping foot block, one foot or the other.

Now copy the monks' other move "Strike ears with your fists". This is what we would call "boxing ears" in the West. Step back, Drop both your hands and then swing your arms out to your sides and behind you. Turn and lift your hands. Move them forward. Close your fists, lift them up and strike your knuckles together in front of you. Don't do it with anyone between those fists. It is quite dangerous. But, playing "Strike Ears with Fists" is a good exercise to test your spirit.

A last kick and the monks finish their exercises. They bow to their teachers, bow and wave to us and return to their various duties. The great round door closes and we go back to our trip along the road down the mountain.

It is warm and sunny going down this side of the ridge. We pick flowers and berries from the shrubs on the sides of the road.

Creep low like a Snake

A snake is sunning himself on the cobbles of the road. Here is a chance to test our defensive Tai Chi. Step out and sweep low to flip the serpent from the road into the weeds without hurting it or, if poisonous, without the snake hurting us.

"Creep low like a snake" is the name of this Tai Chi move.

"Creeping Low" takes practice. It needs and develops leg strength and flexibility to do it well. It is a beautiful and impressive to see done well. On this our gentle Tai Chi trip we decide to try "Creeping Low" some other time and leave the snakes alone today.

From down the end of the road come sounds of laughing and singing. The sounds rise up from the village below. We walk down past the houses and stores until we see where the songs come from.

The Village of Fair Maiden Weavers

In the center square of a village the women have come, as they do each fine day. They have set up their tall wooden weaving looms. They work together, enjoying the company and activity. Each weaves the patterns of the district and of their own family. These were taught to them by their mothers and grandmothers. They will pass them on to their daughters. All can have work in this thriving valley village. The ladies throw their shuttles back and forth full of coloured wool, cotton and silk. Their activity inspires the tai chi moves called" Fair Maidens Throw Weaving Shuttles".

The men of the village? They are on the river or in the fields. But some sit in the square talking politics, drinking wine, tea, playing chess and smoking. The women will relax in the evening. The older children are mostly in school learning. Modern China is moving up the rivers and valleys. The younger children are in baskets or they laugh and play among the looms.

'The Fair Ladies Throw Shuttles" is a good exercise for turning your hips. The looms are large. The ladies need to throw the shuttles strongly to send them over among the warp threads. Each picks up the shuttle, holds it level on one side, then throws. Each throw moves the shuttle all the way across to the other side, keeping it level, steadying it with the other hand. On the other side, they change the shuttle to their other hands and throw the shuttle back. You change the colors of your cloth by changing the shuttles or the patterns by manipulating the vertical woof threads attached to the looms.

The ladies work long and hard. They chat and laugh and sing as they work. Each has her own family patterns. Some teach their daughters on smaller looms beside them.

We watch. You can try throwing some shuttles. But then a bell rings. Their daughters and grandmothers bring tea around. The fair ladies of the village stop for a tea break with us. We can buy a blanket or a bright scarf if we wish.

But soon it is time for the ladies to return to work and for us to return home. The village of the fair maiden weavers is across the river from our own village. We walk away from the village square over to the small dock on the river's edge.

The river here is as wide as a lake. It reflects the hills and mountains above it.

Across the River

At the village dock a fisherman offers to sail us across. As he rows out into the current he tells us to pick up fishing roads. "There are lots of fish in our river".

Fish fill these rivers that run clear from the mountains. Downstream, it is sad to know, as has happened all over the world, among the fields, factories and cities of this modern world, in spite of as much care as possible, there will be fewer fish and the waters will not be so clear. In other places great hydroelectric dams back up the waters from the hills.

We pick up fishing rods, bait hooks and throw out the lines as the fisherman rows us out onto the river. Soon we have caught the fine silver carp. Our fishing is like another Tai Chi move.

"Reaching for the Golden Needle at the Bottom of the Sea"

Our fishing lines go deep down into the water.

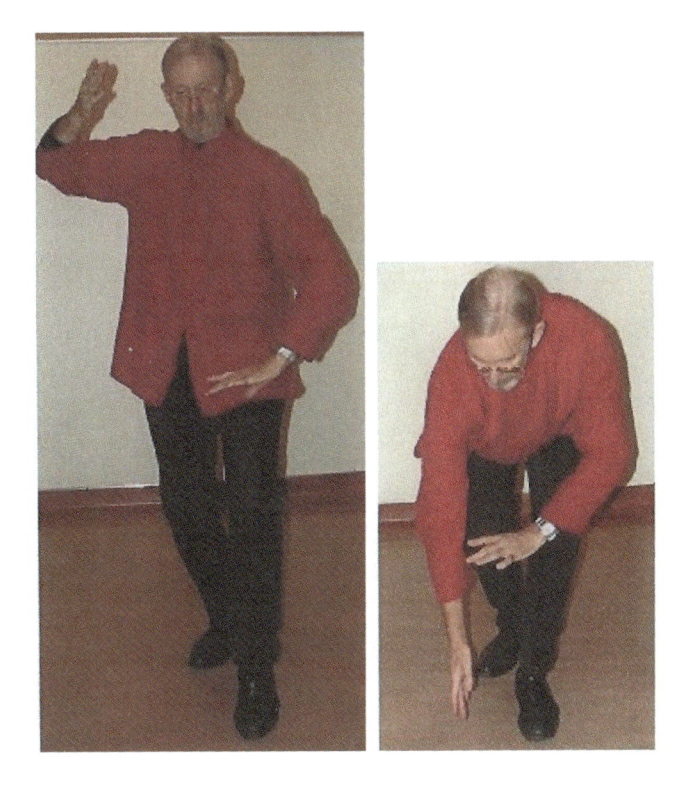

"Reaching for the Golden Needle at the Bottom of the Sea" is the name of the sitting, bending and reaching down of the next Tai Chi move that is part of our story.

The name of these movements come from the story of legendary heroes Sandy, Pigsy and Monkey King who reached down for golden needles in the bottom of the ocean. The fisherman, like many of the older people of China, knows about the "Journey to the West", the 1400 year old legend of the priest who went to India to bring back the sutras of the Buddha to China. That is how Buddhism came into China and became one of the three great religions of China along with the Taoism based on the poems of Lao Tsu's "Tao Te Ching' and the followers of the great teacher, Confucius, that are all still remembered and respected in modern China.

In that good old story the name of Buddha's priest was Xuanzang. When Heaven inspired him on his quest, he was given the heroes, Sandy, Pigsy and mischievous Monkey King, to help him.

Especially, the Monkey King had golden needles which became soldiers when they were brought up from the ocean to fight off bad spirits.

This story gave its name to our next Tai Chi move. To get the golden needles requires reaching down low into the ocean and rising up, lifting them.

In our Monkey Mountain story, we pick up our fishing rod and throw out our lines deep into the lake. Soon we should catch us some of the fine silver carp that fill these rivers.

" How big are your fish?" the fisherman asks us as we bring our fish on deck. We can show off their fine length with another Tai Chi move.

Open the Fan

Cross your hands in front of you with the palms toward your face. Open your hands apart, turning your hands out in the Tai Chi move, "Opening the Fan". Our arms open like big fans to show the length of the fine fish we have caught. The little fish we throw back.

Because he liked this move so much, my young South China Tai Chi teacher, Gwang Ya, had us do "Opening the Fan" three times. First we measure our fish. Then, stretching our arms up, we raise the sails of the fishing boat. Opening for the third time, our crossed hands open to describe the broad smooth river which we now sail across. The smooth water under our bow reflects the blue sky, the green hills and the mountains beyond.

We cross the river. As we approach the far shore, beside our village dock, the fisherman points out the wide bed of lotuses that float among their round green lilly pads near the dock of our village.

Here we will tell the Fisherman's stories about the lotuses to add to our Monkey Mountain story.

These stories and the beautiful Tai Chi moves that go with them come from my friend and Master of Energy Tai Chi Peter Kun Yang's "Old Traditional Tai Chi Set" that I play with him and his students in the Oak Forests of High Park in Toronto, Canada.

As we pass the lotus bed, our fisherman raises his arms to the sky and explains; "Those leaves take the Yang energy of the sun that shines on them all day, down their stems to their roots in the mud deep under the water. There, in the mud and in the roots below, is the Ying energy, that rises up from the earth. It joins and is warmed by the Yang energy of the sun."

"Each day, green buds grow and rise up from the roots and the mud. They spear up through the surface of the water. In the afternoon, they burst open as great new lotus flowers."

Like the fisherman, we become a lotus plant. Our hands collect the sunshine and send the Yang energy down into our feet crossed on the floorboards of his boat. These are the roots of the lotus plants in the mud below. Down low, we put our hands together. They become the green buds growing up from the roots and mud below, through the waters to burst open into pink lotus blossoms.

A dragonfly sits on a lotus. It opens its wings and buzzes off, flying over the river towards a small island.

The fisherman points across the river. "Over there to the south, see that great rock by the island. There is a dark cave beneath it where the mountain cliffs come straight down into the water. That is the cave of the Yang dragon."

The Yang dragon, the fisherman explains to us, collects all the Yang energy of the sun that shines down all day into the river and the lake."

"Sometimes the dragon springs out at a passing boat to remind us of his power. It has a great scaly head. Its body is covered with golden scales. It has a lashing tail of spines. His roar is like the thunder. " The fisherman takes a deep breath and roars. "Ha, Ha, that is good for your lungs"

And then raising his arms from his sides, the fisherman waves his arms. He becomes a great white bird, bigger than any eagle, that flies down from the mountain cliffs over the lake by the island.

"That's the phoenix." says the fisherman storyteller. "The bird is the phoenix of Ying energy. It flies here from the deepest valleys of the highest mountains. It has a roost over there on those cliffs above the dragon cave. When it lands, it shakes its great tail. From that tail come all the colors of the rainbow. It is all the colours of the flowers and the birds and the animals that fall from it into the waters of the lake."

Ying is the energy from the earth itself that makes the green plants grow, that feeds all the birds and fish and animals that feed us. The Ying of the earth and the phoenix mixes with the Yang of the sun and the dragon. Together they make all of life.

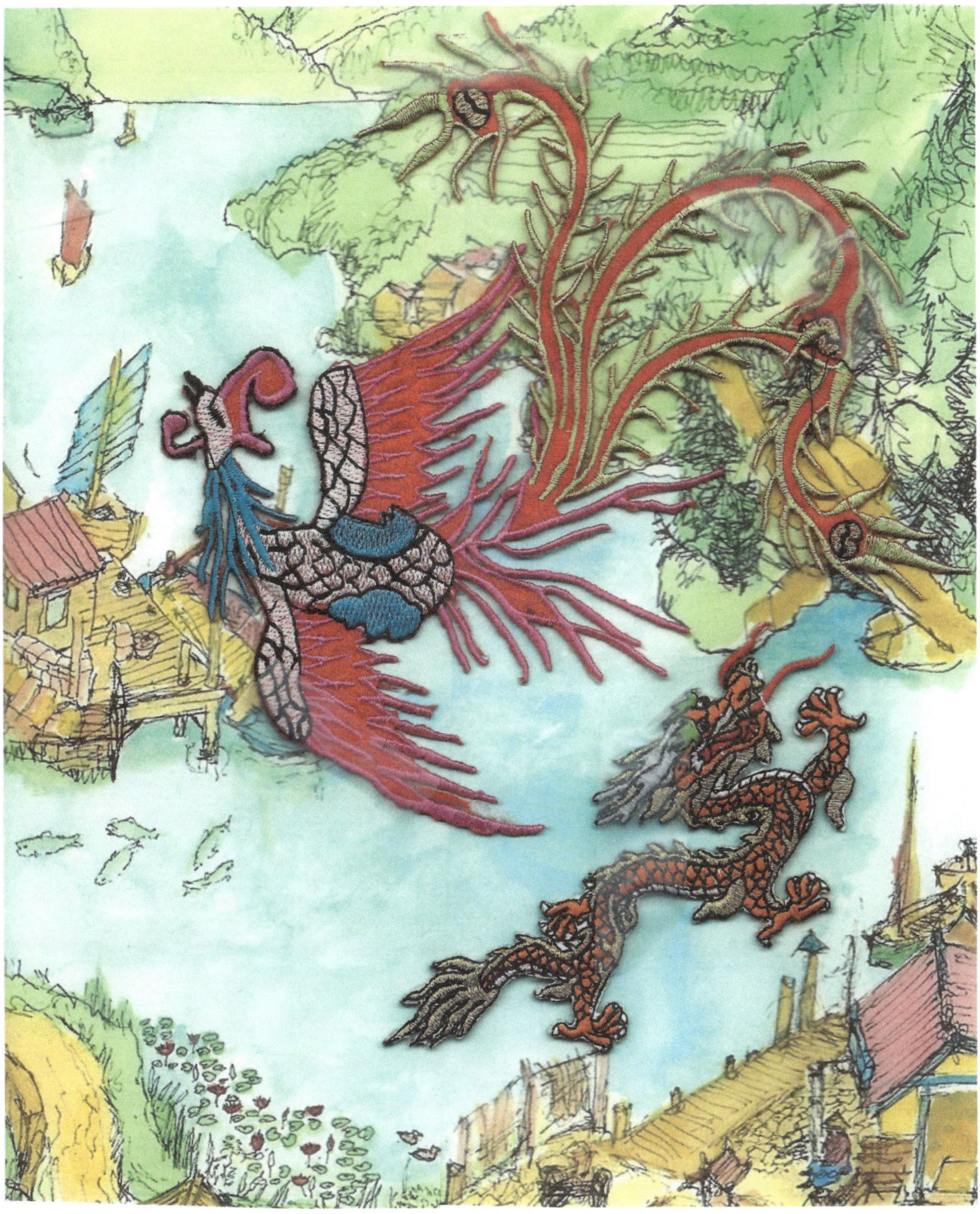

To finish this part of our story, we follow the moves of Peter Yang`s Old Traditional Set. The fisherman leads. He stretches out his arms, opens his hands, presses his index fingers into his palms at the base of his thumbs. He closes his fists and pushes down. Here we can follow this fisherman leader into different kind of Tai Chi movements.

" Press your middle finger into your palm, close your fists and push down. Some of you can feel the energy rise up your back from the bowl of energy within you. It will flow down your shoulders and arms through your hands to the point in the centre of your palms. As you push your finger into the point, the "Chee" energy rises up your arms and goes into your heart. Press hard. Relax and feel the energy and warmth in your body and your spirit". His story and this short set is done.

The fisherman lowers the sails. "I'll have to row back with the current, Goodbye". He looks over the side of the boat where the first pink and red of petals are appearing from the green buds of the lotuses.

We climb up from the dock. The fisherman's boat moves off across the river. We are heading home with our fish and the cloth we bought in the village of the fair maiden weavers across the river. But there are some more moves in our story and our Tai Chi.

The Woodsman, Chop Kindling, Saw off New Wood Block

Beside the dock is the woodsman. He is old and friendly. He has blocks of wood cut from dead trees from the forests above for sale. And he has a small axe.

"Chop yourself some kindling", he tells us.

"Turn and Chop with your fist" is the name of the Tai Chi move. When you repeat this move, it is like chopping kindling from a block. The block is of nice soft pine wood. The chopping and splitting it is easy.

"Please cut off another block for my next customer", says the woodsman.

He hands us his old saw. The sawing is like another Tai Chi move. "Punch with your Fist". Your fist holds the saw. Punch, rasp and pullback. Oriental saws cut on the pull back. Western saws cut on the push. Soon we are done cutting our block. The woodsman thanks us. We pay for our kindling. We gather it up with the fish and the bright coloured cloth from the village across the river.

Home, the Conclusion of the Tai Chi and the Story

We are home. Put the cloth from the village of the weaving maidens, the fish from the river, the kindling from the woodsman, down at the kitchen table.. The trip to the Monkey Mountain is complete. You have done the full Tai Chi set and more.

You can bow to greet your family.

We can do three more Tai Chi bows. The first of these bows will be because we remember all the long tradition that has gone into this art called Tai Chi. Legends speak of 13 "heavenly movements" done by Taoist monks before written history, These became the 108 movements to which the legendary Taoist monk Cheung San Feng gave the name Tai Chi. There are two Chinese written characters for Tai Chi or more correctly, Taiji. 太極.

Tai means the farthest, the highest, the most subtle. Chi, the way we say it in the west or more correctly, Ji, means the natural breath of life. The Chinese speak of animals as naturally having or being Tai Chi. New born babies are also Tai Chi. We are doing this would like to be Tai Chi or Tai Ji.

There are other more profound and subtle meanings for Tai Chi. These meanings are related to the ancient principles of life which the Chinese of legends called the Tao which in English is called "The Way". Tai Chi also is the name of the sets of exercises or movements like the ones we have described on this trip up Monkey Mountain. Often, in China's long history, when times were bad and strength was needed, Tai Chi was found and revived. We also do our first bow for this long tradition.

Our second bow is to our leader for the story up the Mountain and for our teacher and to you and our friends and sisters and brothers that joined us doing this Tai Chi or taking this trip up the Mountain. They share what they know and enjoy working together with us.

And finally you bow to yourself.

When you do Tai Chi, for each move there is your mind, that intelligently seeks health and balance. There is your heart that puts emotion and willpower, fast or gentle, into your actions. Finally there is the energy in you. This is the chee in all life. As in all life, great and small, it rises up into your movements, from your Tan Tien, your center of energy, which Chinese physiology sees in your lower abdomen, centred inside you below your navel. This energy rests and works quietly until it is needed. It comes from the mixing of Ying and Yang energies.

In doing Tai Chi you are also your own leader. You have respected the past, respected and followed your family and teacher. This last bow is to express your concern and respect for yourself, for your health and all that you have in this world. This is the third bow.

As my first Tai Chi teacher, Master Moy Lin Shin said when we asked him what was the right way to live, what was the Tao of life. " Rise up, do your job, climb your mountain, come home, enjoy your friends and family".

Thank you for joining me on the trip up Monkey Mountain. I hope you have enjoyed it and it has made you feel good. It is my sincere hope you will take your own trips up the Mountain and maybe lead your friends with you.

The End

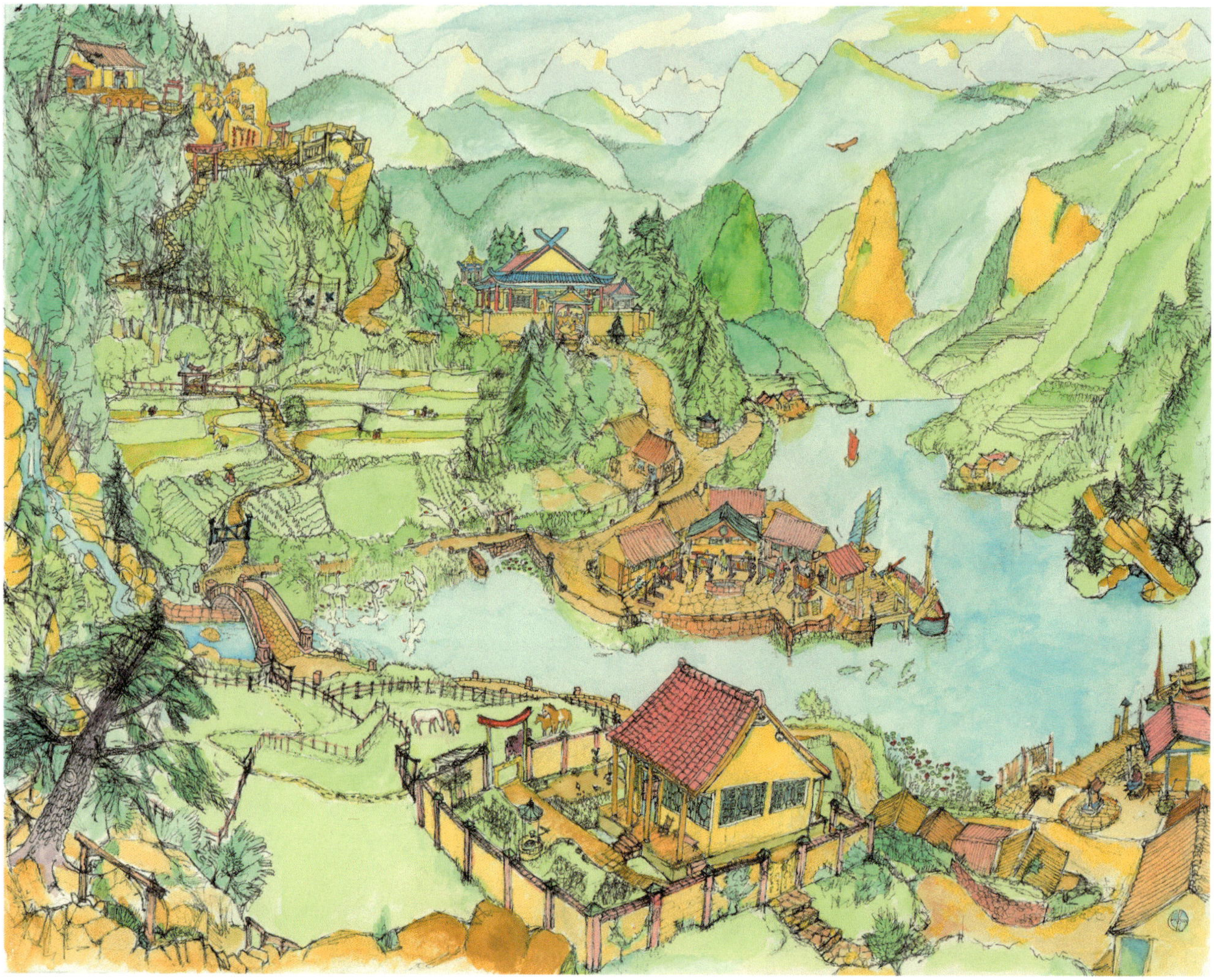

Chapter 3:

A Short Preface about Tai Chi, the Trip up Monkey Mountain and Monkey Mountain Story Tai Chi

The Story about the Story ---

You have this book about Tai Chi and a new kind of Tai Chi.

Each of us finds Tai Chi in our own way. Mine was discovering the Chinese philosophy classic, the "Tao Te Ching". It was D. C. Lau's "Tao Te Ching" a Penguin Book published in 1963. I first saw these poems in an airport in Chicago. Not long after, I was told there was a kind of Yoga that studied the ideas of the Tao Te Ching and that it was called Tai Chi. That was back in 1972.

Now, forty or more years later, the ideas about the natural way of life and the exercise that are based on those poems remain important to me. I have placed an old man, I hope like the man who wrote the poems of the "Tao Te Ching", on top of the Monkey Mountain ridge in this new way of doing Tai. When you go up there I hope you will discover some of the things that I have discovered learning and teaching Tai Chi. As many as possible of those ideas are in the trip up Monkey Mountain.

In the same way that I and other fellow students began to lead and teach Tai Chi when we first learned it from Master Moy, I hope that some of you will also help to lead others up the mountain to do Tai Chi.

Different Tai Chi's and Monkey Mountain

There are many different styles or ways to do Tai Chi from all over the far east. Today they have spread around the world. They are played by many, many thousands of people of all ages in North and South America, Europe and every continent.

The Tai Chi I first found had 108 moves to learn. The Tai Chi set behind the Monkey Mountain story is the short, or 24 move form of the classical Yang style of Tai Chi. The legendary story of the start of Yang Style Tai Chi was that a young man lived with a family called Wu which practiced and guarded their own Tai Chi. The old master gave young Yang permission to teach and spread Tai Chi to the capital of the empire of China at that time. He was a great success. All over China this Tai Chi was called Yang's Tai Chi.

Modern classical Yang style Tai Chi is credibly traced back to a revival of Tai Chi in the troubled times of the late 19th Century in central China (ref. 3; Douglas Wile "Lost Tai Chi Classics from the late Ching Dynasty", SUNY Press, 1996). The short form of Yang Tai Chi became popular after the people of most of China adopted communism as their way of government in 1948. It is now done by more people around the world than any other formal exercise.

Chee and Chi Kung in Tai Chi and the Monkey Mountain Story

When I did this Sun Rises movement early in my Tai Chi training Master Moy asked me, "What do you feel?" in his broken English. I said I felt an energy flow inside me. "That is chee"Master Moy answered.

I learned that what I was feeling was what the Chinese perceived as the energy of life that acts in our bodies and in all living things. The Chinese have names for all of these places in our bodies that form part of their traditional learnings of physiology, their anatomy for of how our bodies work. This energy also is understood to move unconsciously throughout our bodies and organs.

From deep in China's history and prehistory, those who studied and understood the movement of energy created the sets of exercises from these feelings and their applications that became Tai Chi. There are stories about monks and masters watching and copying the movement of animals to understand the movement of energy. Traditionally these became the original 108 moves in the Tai Chi set, from which other Tai Chis and Tai Chi sets were made into the sets of 18 or 43, or 64 or 24 moves or forms. In many of these, like in the Monkey Mountain story, new moves could be added and tried out.

There is also an intense study and art of the movement of chee throughout our bodies. It is known as Chi or Chee Kung,. This knowledge is then applied to the proper functioning of our organs and for different conditions of our bodies. Chee energy informs the traditional practices of Acupuncture, acupressure and moxibustion, and the Chinese medical pharmacy of diet, of herbs and materials, long used in Chinese medicine.

Tai Chi, over the ages, has also been moved by this knowledge. All of this, including Tai Chi and Chee Kung, is beginning, tentatively, to be studied medically and scientifically in the rest of the world, even as many westerners accept and enjoy its benefits.

Doing this story, learning, studying and trying these new ideas are the parts of Tai Chi that also help us to clear and enlighten our minds, and as the writer Confucius wrote, make our wills sincere. We can then go on to use this knowledge to improve our lives and our health. our families and our communities. The story and Tai Chi lead us to follow what the other ancient traditional Chinese teacher, Confucius' advised was the way of the elders to achieve peace and prosperity in the world.

Monkey Mountain is a little story inspired by Tai Chi to help, if only a little, here where we are far from China and China's history.

The other meanings of "Tai Chi".

The Tai Chi that we are talking about in this story is the name for an exercise. The exercise Tai Chi is the "Sets of moves or movements" that go into the Monkey Mountain story. This is one of the meanings of many meanings of "Tai Chi".

We say that we do or play Tai Chi exercises. This is sometimes called Tai Chi Chuan. The Chuan means boxing. This emphasizes the martial arts, protective or defensive ways of moving your body or your limbs which are part of Tai Chi. The Monkey Mountain story is a kind of Tai Chi Chuan.

Tai Chi has other multidimensional and subtle meanings beyond or behind the studies and the exercises called Tai Chi or Tai Chi boxing. "Tai Chi", if you look at the two characters that make up the Chinese word, seems to mean "extreme moving". "Tai" is a simple word meaning far out or extreme. "Tai Bei" in Chinese is the farthest north, the North Pole. "Chi" in the word Tai Chi is a far more complex word character itself. Some Tai Chi teachers speak of the natural quality of animals as being Tai Chi. Animals move naturally for their purposes. Cats especially exhibit this naturalness of moving. Fluid, we call it. And we have it too.

Tai Chi is also the Chinese name for the natural perfection of life. Our Tai Chi, our exercise and our story, try to be as close as can be to this natural Tai Chi. It could also be seen as the expression of the results of evolution of all forms of life. Tai Chi is the better ways of moving that we learn as we advance in the exercises called Tai Chi. Learning the movements of Tai Chi is taking advantage of thousands of years of study of how beautifully our bodies work.

For us humans, as a species of animal, Tai Chi exists when we are babies. We all can see the natural perfection of babies. My first teacher, Master Moy used to fill with pleasure and animation when someone brought a young infant into the room. He would insist on holding the baby. He would lay it along his forearm gently, its head at his elbow, steadying it with the other hand. "Feel that chee." he would say, beaming.

So, the beginning of Tai Chi, the Sun Rises, in the Monkey Mountain story and in a Tai Chi set, is the beginning of your experiencing Tai Chi. It may also be your first experience of the energy and movements within your body that the Chinese have given the name Chi or " chee", the name for something that some have studied very seriously, but which comes naturally as part of your study of Tai Chi.

The Beginning of the Monkey Mountain Story and Tai Chi

Monkey Mountain Tai Chi started in Canada in 1999. It uses the 24 moves of the Short Form of Classical Yang Tai Chi as taught by Master Zu Gwang Ya, a teacher who visited Canada in the early 1990's from Nanjing in southeastern China. It also uses moves taught by Dr. Peter Yang, a Chinese medical doctor and acupuncturist who learned Tai Chi in Shanghai before coming to Germany and now Toronto, Canada. Moves from their sets and from Tai Chi master Moy Lin Shin, who taught in Toronto from the late 1960's are used or sometimes modified in the Monkey Mountain Story. His Taoist Tai Chi was specially designed for health.

Some years later I learned the short form of Yang Tai Chi from Ju Gwang Ya, a young Chinese history of architecture professor who was visiting Canada. He had rebuilt a garden in south China and told a story about a poem carved on a rock wall in the garden. The poem was written by two young lovers, soon to be separated forever by China's history, but preserved in the garden that the young professor had repaired. The rock and the poem are now up at the Monkey Mountain lookout.

The Tai Chi classes at South Riverdale Community Health Center began in Toronto in 1996. The Seniors Wellness class members there were my teachers for the next ten years. We learned how difficult it is to learn the Tai Chi set, even just 24 moves, when you start after 60 years old.

This was when the Monkey Mountain story came into our Tai Chi. A story was a way to make the moves and the sequence of the Tai Chi exercises familiar, easier to remember and easier to follow. At the same time it was possible for the leader, sometimes me sometimes Tai Chi teacher, Mrs Tzu Ho Hong, to go into the details of each of the Tai Chi and the Monkey Mountain moves. We all improved as repetition and increasing practice made us stronger, better balanced and more confident. We even tried the traditional Tai Chi game of Push Hands and together learned about using and relaxing the internal energy in our bodies, the beginning of the Chinese study called Chi Kung. The stuffed pony, the bell, the music, the monkeys, fish, became part of the story. Finally, a picture of Monkey Mountain was painted.

2006, The members of the South Riverdale Community Health Center Senior Wellness Class

Since then, the Monkey Mountain story has made it possible to introduce Tai Chi into hospitals, nursing homes, psychological therapy, diabetic treatment programs and community residential drop in programs. In most of these programs there was little time to use the usual progressive teaching of Tai Chi or even short sets of moves. The Monkey Mountain story was simple enough that people in all sorts of places and those with considerable disabilities, or in wheelchairs could try and follow most of the movements of the Tai Chi set. They enjoy the story and benefit from the movements. It is now time to tell this story to a lot more people.

Chapter 4

The 27 Tai Chi Moves of the Monkey Mountain Story

Why do we make the trip up Monkey Mountain. And why is this trip especially good for you, whoever you are, old or young?

The answer is in the moves of Tai Chi. The value is also in the way you learn the Tai Chi moves.
These are the moves you follow and learn at each of the 15 Stations in the Monkey Mountain Story. They are done on each trip up Monkey Mountain. In the Monkey Mountain story, these are the 24 Moves that come from the moves taught the world over as the Short Yang Style Tai Chi. Near the end of the story there are also two moves from the "Old Traditional Tai Chi Set" taught by Dr. Peter Kung Yang in Toronto,'s High Park.

Some of the Monkey Mountain Story moves are variations of the Yang style moves but the Yang moves they mimic are easily taught and are described here.

On Monkey Mountain and in the story there are 15 stations you pass as you go up and down the Mountain. Each station is for learning and practicing one or more of the 24 Tai Chi moves, until you experience or know them all!

Each player of Tai Chi learns these moves by following a leader, a teacher or as they are called in China, a master, who in turn has learned them following his or her teachers. All have learned by watching, copying and then feeling the moves in themselves. Before the historical teachers of Tai Chi and the different modern styles, there was the legend of the Taoist Monk and teacher, Cheung San Feng, "Three Valley Cheung", who gave Tai Chi its name. And before him were stories of other Taoist or just natural legendary players and teachers and exercises. One early name written about was "The Thirteen Heavenly Movements". But the tradition of copying, learning and feeling goes on and on.

When you begin to play Tai Chi, you learn how to do each move, not just once but many times. These moves then may become your moves, to remember and repeat. The moves you have learned will also change as your strength, your balance, your knowledge and your confidence grow. Tai Chi depends very much on your knowledge and your spirit as it did with the spirit of each of your teachers before you to lead you.

You can get ideas from reading about these moves. But reading cannot replace the learning passed from teachers to students. "What did you learn from that book? How long did it take to read? How long have you been doing Tai Chi with me?", said my first teacher. That was after about ten years learning with Master Moy.

Monkey Mountain story itself is an exception in the teaching of Tai Chi. This is just a story. You can hear it and remember it. You can play the story in your imagination and then you will fit your own Tai Chi moves that you learn into the story.

If you also learn other traditional or classical Tai Chi and Tai Chi sets and their moves you can fit these moves and ideas into the story. But here to begin, join me and let me tell you some of what I have learned about each of the moves that are part of this Monkey Mountain story. We will begin at the beginning at the cottage in the village.

In the Morning, outside the back door of of the Cottage

Station 1 of the Monkey Mountain Story

First Movement of the 24 ;

In this section, a few of the moves will be shown in photographs, but only a few. It is by working with a teacher or leader that you will learn all of the moves, and how they can be done. Later you might also go deeper into each move. This is how one "masters" Tai Chi. Here we are just beginning, but the benefits start from now.

1. **"The Sun Rises".**   In the beginning of your trip up Monkey Mountain you do the moves called "The Sun Rises". This is the essential traditional beginning of Tai Chi, and of all Tai Chi sets. The move is simple. Raise both your arms until your finger tips are as high as your shoulders and lower them. You do it slowly.

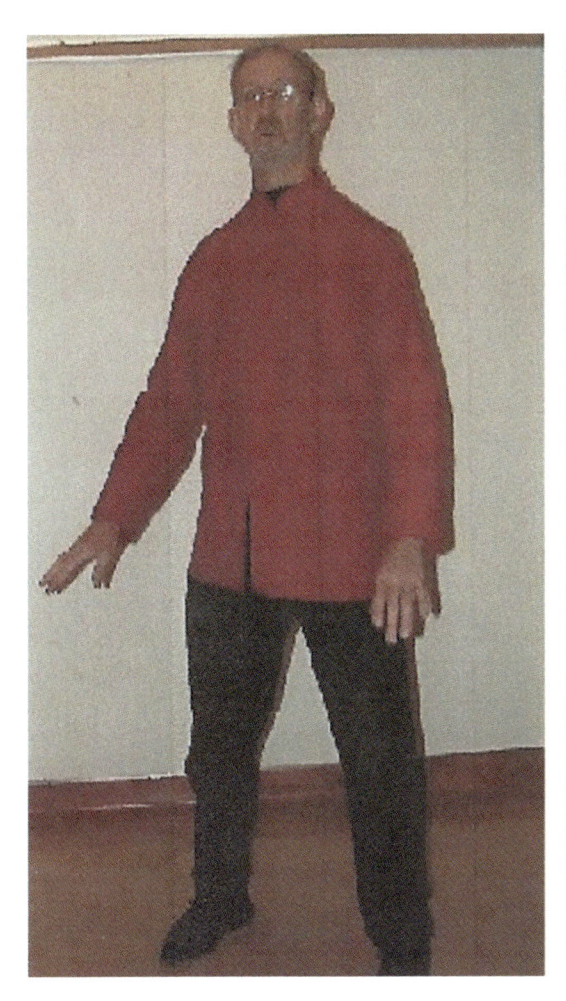

Or, with your hands down by your knees, lift and extend your fingers as if the sun was resting on them. Now raise the sun up. This will put your will into the sun rising, especially to do it slowly. Energy will rise up your spine. The energy in your back, shoulders and arms will do the work of rising like the sun.

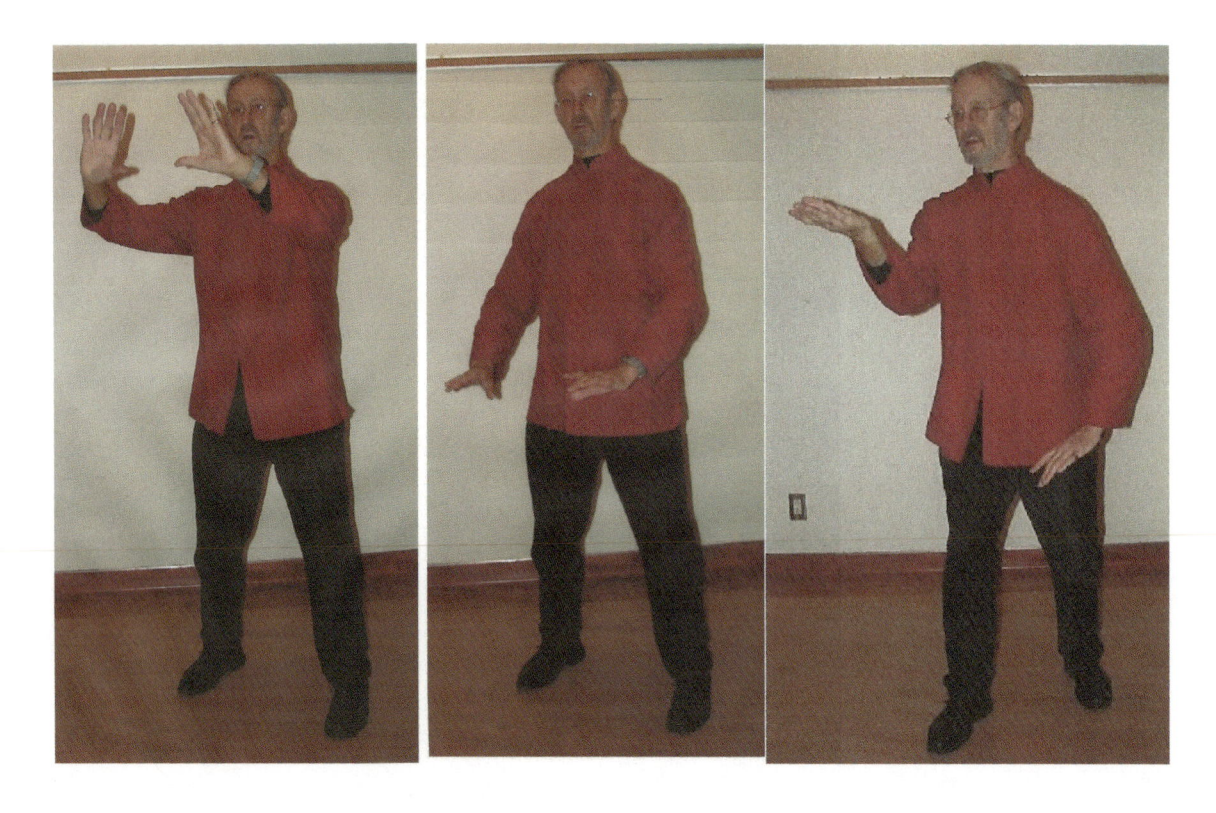

Lifting the Sun, Shining Down.

Once up, leave your arms and the sun up there. Relax your shoulders. Feel you whole body relax. You may feel the energy relax also. Your arms stay up. Muscles other than those around your shoulders that did the raising up, take over. But the energy, or the "something", that in China is called chi or chee, that powered your arms up, is relaxed and seems to flow down from your shoulders through your chest, to rest in your abdomen. The Chinese have a name for this area in your abdomen. It is called, the lower tan tien, the lower center of your energy, the bowl or cradle of your chee. This explanation is for the real feeling that is experienced in the first move of your story and of the Tai Chi set. It is important. It is the beginning of learning Tai Chi.

Push down, lowering your arms, slowly and gently. This could be the sun shining down on the garden, the flowers, the vegetables as the story says, even on the chickens in the yard. And with your hands back at your knees, relax again. The same energy, the same 'something" will move again in you, relaxing. The energy returns again to your lower center of energy. Try the sun rises and lowers again. It will be the same.

**The Ponies in the Field,
Monkey Mountain** Station 2

Second group of Movements.

Combing the Wild Horse's Mane, to the left and to the right, is the second set of moves of the Short Yang Tai Chi set. In the Monkey Mountain Set, the Yang Tai Chi moves become "Saddle up the pony, and ride over to the base of the Mountain". Now we begin the Tai Chi work with other parts of our bodies.

It is said that doing Tai Chi protects you from accidental falls. The exercise's effectiveness for this has been researched and documented all over the world and the results can be easily found on the internet. Tai Chi players also report that tripping becomes less frequent in day to day walking, and recovery from near falls improves. I believe that these effects come from learning the Tai Chi way of walking. This we learn by taking our ponies over to the base of the mountain which will be used in many of the other series of movements in Yang and Monkey Mountain Tai Chi.

Jogging is extreme walking. Marathoning is even more extreme. These are for the younger and those more energetically ambitious to increase their leg and body strength and lung and cardiac endurance. Tai Chi sets a more reasonable pace. The Tai Chi walking or riding the pony over to the mountains and then for climbing the mountain is different to ordinary walking.

Tai Chi walking is more like what the Sufi master Georgi Gurdjieff taught 90 years ago. He was trying to lead a group of his young students safely out of the Bolshevik, White Russian war zone through the thick woods on a moonless night. His lesson sounds very much like Tai Chi walking. In the trip up Monkey Mountain story there is the description of learning this Tai Chi walking. It is what you begin to learn at the second station, riding the ponies over to the mountain.

In my first years learning the practice of the 108 movement Tai Chi set, a lot of time and energy was devoted to strengthening the leg muscles. There were special sitting exercises. Warmup exercises loosened and stretched the ligaments of knees, thighs, calves and ankles and built up the muscles to make it possible to easily lift and lower the weight of the body, whether one was large or small, heavy or light. If heavier people practiced hard they became that much stronger and became really good Tai Ch players.

Then these improvements are practiced in all of the Tai Chi sets' movements.

Monkey Mountain Tai Chi and the story make this walking a most important part of learning and participating. But even before learning to climb Monkey Mountain, older people can begin learning Tai Chi with one of the most useful and simple added exercise. Get up out of a chair using and feeling your leg muscles. New students, even those with sore, damaged or arthritic knees, weak thighs and more than enough weight are encouraged, insistently recommended, to get up and sit back down, preferably as slowly as possible, at least five times a day. An arm chair will help at first. Soon this can become ten times, as your legs grow stronger. Tai Chi sets become easier, more steady, balanced and more elegant. Life becomes easier and safer.

Different Tai Chi styles teach different details to the Tai Chi walking at first. But behind them all is the principle, right from the start, of using the turning of the waist to move the body's weight from one leg to the other. For the younger and stronger, one can increase the slowness and deepness of sitting and stretch out the legs further in each step. Try it a few times and you will see how much strength it requires.

One can also climb three Monkey Mountains, using the short Yang Tai Chi's 24 movements three times, to come closer to the regular 108 movement of traditional Tai Chi sets.

As described in the Story, the movements of riding your Pony across the fields is done by "Combing the Wild Horse's Mane". You step forward and raise your hand in front of you as in the illustration above, and as if you were combing the stiff mane of the pony you were riding.

To ride your pony down the field and across to the bridge at the base of the mountains you will repeat this "combing" each time to take a Tai Chi step forward. Three of these movements, right, left and right again, combing each time is enough for the story.

After the slow careful walking movements, "riding" across the fields, the next movements are a welcome change. This second movement, riding to the mountain, and later, the fourth movement, Carrying a Tiger to the Mountain are the movements of the Tai Chi set that make the legs become stronger with each set played, each trip taken up the mountain.

The Bridge and the White Cranes.
Station 3 of Monkey Mountain

3. "The White Cranes Cool Their Wings" is the name of the third movement of the Monkey Mountain set.

     The White Cranes cooling their wings is attractive, enjoyable, even amusing, as a dance move and as an exercise. As a dance move it captures the visual and creative imagination of imitating the big birds. The movements of all animals impressed and inspired the inventors of Tai Chi and of other kinds of Chinese exercises, but the cranes did so particularly. The interpretation of the cranes can be about peace and gentle elegance. It can also be the expression of strength and rivalry. To watch the cranes or the players cooling their wings at Tai Chi can also be a bit ludicrous as they learn.

     As an exercise, imitating the cranes' movements is a test of flexibility in the arms and shoulders. Cranes cooling their wings is done differently in different styles of Tai Chi. It can begin with a step and a push to one side, followed by a half step up and then a strong spiraling up with the upper hand. Monkey Mountain follows the classical Yang Tai Chi's gentler step forward, step up on one toe and stretch. It can be done for maximum stretch or for elegance of appearance.

In the usual set it is done just once, right left foot forward. I was told that this was because of subtle movement of chee in this move. Usually I repeat the stretching up on both sides for the flexibility and joy of the movement. In years to come or when I meet that subtle master I might learn the internal subtelties of this elegant move.

It is a surprise that very few people have difficulty doing "Cranes Cool Their Wings". This energetic and unique mimicking movement is also a demonstration of Tai Chi's naturalness and effectiveness as a stretching exercise. It is one of the most exhilarating of Tai Chi's movements and images.

Leaving the cranes dancing and feeding by the lowlands and marshes along the great river, it is now time to climb the hillside of the Monkey Mountain Ridge. It is also time to learn the strong pushing movements that begin Tai Chi's use of defensive actions as part of the set.

Climbing Monkey Mountain Ridge
Station 4

4. "Carry the Tiger up the Mountain" in the Yang Tai Chi set is " Protect your knees, turn and carry the tiger up the mountain". In the Monkey Mountain story this becomes "Climb the mountain, through the farmers' gate, carrying a little tiger cub, up past the fields, gardens and the rice paddies on the lower part of the mountain, through another gate and up among the trees, then up to the Monkey Mountain ridge and Lookout".

"Carrying a tiger up the mountain" seems excessive imagery. It expresses how to put weight and energy into these movements and into the pushing arms which simulates the climb up the mountain in this move. The "Carrying a tiger " hand form and movement is somewhat like holding your hand out of the window in a speeding car and catching the wind in your palm. When you imagine you are holding a tiger in your palm, the lift becomes more real.

One of the principles of Chinese philosophy and of Tai Chi is of the balance of opposing and opposite energies. Action and reaction would be an example of this. In the body, both hands can push forward. But if one hand pushes forward, that push will become firmer if the other hand pushes back. In a Tai Chi move this is often the answer for what you do with the other hand.

Climb the mountain (with your tiger) with one hand and the other hand pushes down beside your knee. It is called "protect your knee" in some practices. This defense actually works if someone in front of your takes a kick at your knee or groin.

In the Monkey Mountain story and Tai Chi, this movement of the "other Hand" is turned into "opening the farmer's gate" which is easier to relate to than the "brush your knee ", which is how the movement of the hand not "climbing the mountain" is taught and described in more traditional Tai Chi.

Step forward, open the gate. Look back and pick up your tiger cub. It is easier to demonstrate than describe. Now your hand moves forward past your ear, going down the path, then rising up. This is the climbing the mountain and your hand in front of you, forgetting the tiger cub for a moment, pushes ahead of you and begins to look and feel like the mountain itself ahead of you.

On the lower slopes of Monkey Mountain, the first of three steps takes you through the gate, up through the lower fields and gardens. You can wave at the people working there! Then it's up along the paths across or around the rice paddies.

The second step, opening another gate, takes you up into the steeper wooded part of the trip up the Monkey Mountain Ridge. As I've already told you in the story, Monkey Mountain is just a ridge running down from the higher hills and real mountains above.

You move your hand, with its tiger cub, up along the path through the woods. You can feel the air getting fresher, hear birds and small animals. This second step will take you up above the trees to where a steeper path and some stone stairs take you to the very top of the ridge.

A third step, perhaps reaching down to clear some branches off this steeper track, will take you and your tiger cub up to the posts and their carved crosstree that announce that you have reached the Monkey Mountain Lookout, the famous Monkey Mountain Lookout. Across the leveled area of the lookout is the wonderful view over the other side of the ridge. And there are another series of Tai Chi moves and some extra events for the Tai Chi set and the story.

The Lookout
Station 5

Movement 5. Step Up and Play The Fiddle.

When you reach the lookout on top of Monkey Mountain, you step forward, step up with the other foot, then sit back and raise both hands in front of you. It is traditionally called **Step Up and Play The Fiddle.** You can also reach back into a pack on your shoulder to take out a musical instrument. Your hands are held as if you were holding a flute or a Chinese single string violin. The sitting back is what makes this Tai Chi move very stable and tests the strength of the leg you are sitting back on.

Sitting back like this is part of "Push-hands", the Tai Chi game of attack and repulse played by two opponents to test their strength, stability and Tai Chi knowledge. Often the one who can sit back lowest will overcome when the other person overextends their push. The sitback is also the basis for the more advanced "Moving Tai Chi Push-hands". Opponents alternately step forward to push and step back to avoid being thrown off balance. It is a fascinating and powerful dance for the players. Push hands will be played again in another series of movements, later in the story and the set; when you will be "grasping the bird's tail". You will have already tried the backwards part of this exercise in "stepping up to play the Fiddle" and now you will use it again in "repulsing the monkeys".

Movement 6.
Step Back and Repulse Monkeys

The monkeys give the name to the story, to the mountain and to this new approach to Tai Chi. **"Step Back and Repulse Monkeys"** and "repulsing the monkeys" are some of the most amusing, enjoyable and unique and effective moves of Tai Chi.

Only in imagination can westerners understand the energy and persistence of our ancient cousins who are worshipped for their pure life-force, complete and yet without our human self-consciousness. They are the raw energy in Tai Chi that must balance the care and slowness of so much of the set. It emphasizes the Yang energy which must work with the gentler but no less powerful energy called Ying, the two forces that together arise out of the Tao and are the root of Tai Chi. The coming of the monkeys adds humor, but not without defensiveness. You step back while pushing forward to keep in touch with your imaginary, energetic adversaries.

The monkeys on the mountain ridge lookout are a main theme of this Tai Chi set and story. Of the many reasons for doing Tai Chi, avoiding being pushed around by persistent external forces is one of the earliest and simplest motivations to learn Tai Chi and become stronger and more stable. Shakespeare's "slings and arrows of outrageous fortune" are more easily and calmly prepared for with a practice like Tai Chi. Backing up can be hazardous itself unless one has worked on it. Backing away from a band of monkeys is a good imaginery way to try it out.

One looks and presses one hand forward to repulse the oncoming monkeys. One also looks back behind to make sure that it is safe to move back.

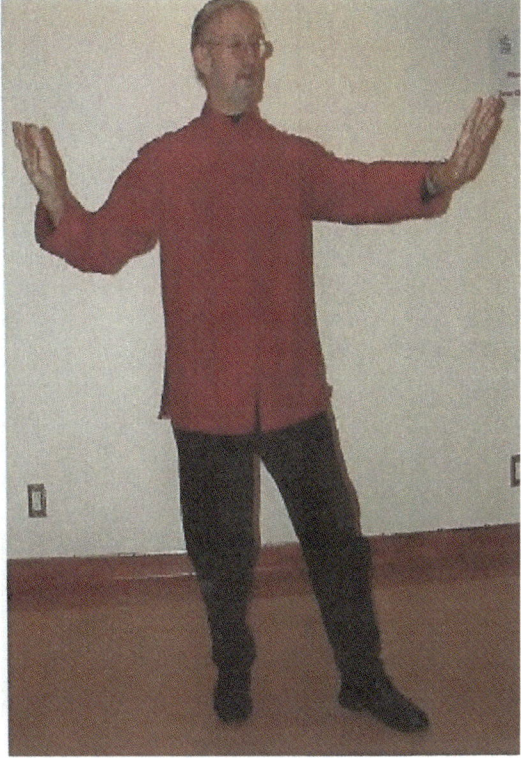

Two things happen. The energy of looking moves from the front to behind and the energy of balance of the weight of your body moves into the back leg. You are more stable, ready to be able to step back with the other foot as the move, or the monkeys, require. The Chinese would add feeling the chee acting in this move. Chee, the complex moving force of our bodies, includes the chee in the eyes moving with the chee in the waist and the legs to change your center of balance.

In China's 5,000 years of history there has been a continual study of the reality of "chee" as a way of understanding the amazing coordination of our bodies. The whole field of Chinese medicine and pharmacy includes learning Tai Chi, and the art and study called Chi or Chee Kung, and the art of acupuncture, the practice of using needles , among other ways, to influence the movement of "Chee". In all these practices there have been long, long study and recorded knowledge of the mind, the heart, the muscles, the organs, heart beat and breathing.

All of these have are today finding their place with the discoveries of the middle eastern, African, and our western world's science, medicine and descriptions of physiology.

Learning Tai Chi One is one way to begin to learn and understand some of Chinese or oriental medical practice. And we are proposing that the entry to Tai Chi is the Monkey Mountain story.

And, here, battling monkeys on this until now beautiful Lookout we must add a special move for the Monkey Mountain story:

The Hermit's Bell Rings.

How can you really repulse the monkeys at the Lookout in our Monkey Mountain story? By luck?

Because this is a story, we can invent a wonderful old hermit who lives high up the ridge. His students bring enough food for him, for them on their visits and for the monkeys. He has trained young monkeys to ring the bell up there when the food is put out for them. In our story the bell rings and away go the monkeys back up the ridge to the hermit's courtyard. There are more ways than one of doing Tai Chi where monkeys are concerned.

I think of the first picture I saw of Lao Tsu, the founder of Taoism on the cover of a Penguin paperback. This book was of his poems. They are the basis of the Chinese idea of Tao which I soon learned was the basis of Tai Chi. Tao is the way that Lao Tsu in his poems in the "Tao Te Ching", The Classic about the Tao and Living its virtue, described that way which has no special name but which was the beginning of all life. In the same way, Tai Chi is the nameless way, the very good exercise way to health and wellness.

Old Lao would be the kind of person who would live alone up on the mountain ridge. There his ideas attract young students and feed the monkeys. That was the kind of person and the kind of ideas that first led me to Tai Chi.

With the monkeys gone we can relax and enjoy the rest of our lunch, or as we do in the Toronto nursing homes, have some tea at the lookout on top of Monkey Mountain. But then we must continue on our ways with our set and the story

The Road Down the Back of the Monkey Mountain Ridge
Station 6

Moves 7 and 8 of the Monkey Mountain Trip:
Free the Songbirds.

There are important moves called **"Grasp the Bird's Tail to the Left** and **to the Right"** in Yang Tai Chi. They are important in Tai Chi because they are the basis for one of the most effective ways of playing Tai Chi, which is called "Push-Hands". These moves have been changed to "freeing the songbirds" in our Monkey Mountain story and trip because they are more aggressive than we need in the story's gentle approach to Tai Chi, but to know the Tai Chi behind the Story, they need to be described.

But first, the Story.

We leave the Lookout and walk down the pathway on the back side of the ridge. As we walk we notice that local villagers have set up some nets in a valley beside the path. This is a common way to catch wild fowl and ducks. It could also be a scientific bird study site. But here there is noone to attend the nets. There are small songbirds, brightly coloured, tangled and struggling in the net. In this Monkey Mountain story set we will "Free the Songbirds from the Birdhunters' nets" and lower the nets.

These movements of the Yang Tai Chi set were the first to be seriously changed for the Monkey Mountain story.

"Grasp the Bird's Tail" are four movements in one in the original 24 move Tai Chi set. These movements are different in form and intention to the "Freeing the Trapped Songbirds" of the Monkey Mountain story. But they are so interesting and important in the learning of Tai Chi that it is worthwhile to describe the original moves in detail.

"Grasping the Bird's Tail" forms the basis of the movements of the Tai Chi game called "Push Hands". This is the practice related to Tai Chi where the real strength and the form of the movements of the set can be tried out hand to hand with a fellow player. Push Hands is done by pairs of players facing off, and to put it simply, trying to push each other off balance.

"Push Hands" is how you learn about the beautiful structure of your body. You learn how to use it in real time under pressure from a determined but respectful opponent who is also learning his or her own real strength. You may also go on to learn the part that chee plays in the strength of your movements. This is far beyond the Monkey Mountain story but you are beginning to feel and learn what it means when you do the story's Tai Chi. Doing Push-Hands will be where you might be lucky enough to find and recognize that real teacher who has advanced into the secrets of Tai Chi and of understanding the way of working, the Tao, of our bodies.

For me this was when Master Moy told me to go "push hands" with young Tony Fong. Master Moy never pushed hands with students. We were not yet ready. Tony was well along to being ready so that in our several months of playing push hands I learned all I know from him. Like my learning Tai

Chi from Tony, the Story's "Freeing the Songbirds" is a good place to begin to experience the Tai Chi of "Grasping the Bird's Tail".

Each part of the Yang Tai Chi "Grasping the Bird's Tail" has a name. The first part of the moves is Peng. This means "to ward off", gently reach out to engage.

Step forward raising one hand to resist, or ward off, a push or protect from a barrier. Done with your elbow low, your arm forming a curve, the back of the one hand facing out, Peng is amazingly firm, even though the whole arm, wrist and hand are relaxed. Your other hand drops down to protects the forward knee, or it is raised up behind and adding support to the other raised hand.

The next part is named Lu, "rolling, pulling back". It is done with both hands reaching in front of you, grasping "the bird's tail" of the opponent's arm and shoulder. Then rolling back, turning to the side and pulling down firmly to that side, using your whole body.

Next is Ji, "cross your hands and press". After the roll back, you once again push ahead of you. This time your hands are crossed to form the strongest curved arch with both your crossed forearms. The natural structure of your shoulders, collarbones, arms, forearms and wrists, linked through your back, send any pressure down to your legs.

Whoever has the firmest stance and the strongest legs will prevail. Well, not always, because if one of the players more profoundly understands where the force and the chee is acting, no matter what the muscles, and the difference in size of bones and body, there will be the greater firmness in the end.

And finally An; Pull your two hands apart. Press down to your sides. Then, the two hand push out ahead of you. Then you may extend your push as far as you can. Now you become the aggressor and the opponent will receive or resist your push in the give and take of "Push Hands". Push Hands can be done using one hand only or the more elaborate two hands, and the ultimate, moving push hands. Then you step forward or back and repeat "Grasping the Bird's Tai" to one or the other side.

We will begin with the simpler movements of "Freeing the Songbirds". Doing them you will find the movements of the hips, arms, hands and legs are similar but gentler. Later you may go on to try "Grasping the Birds Tail" and Push hands.

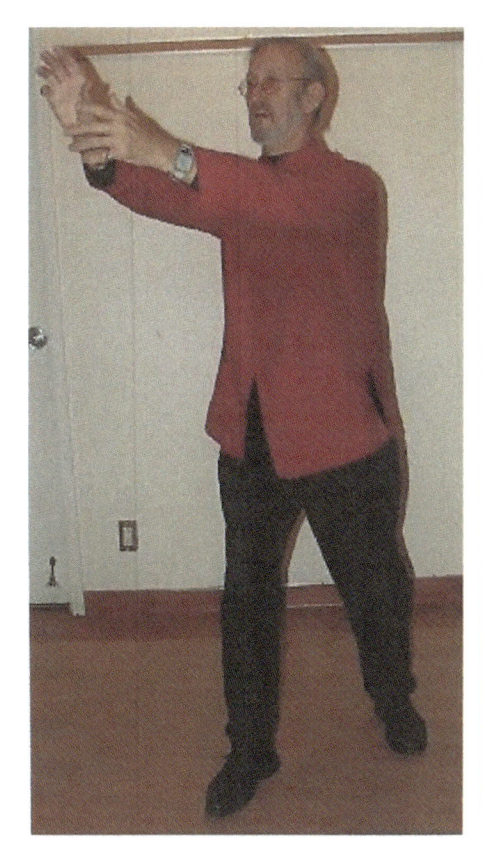

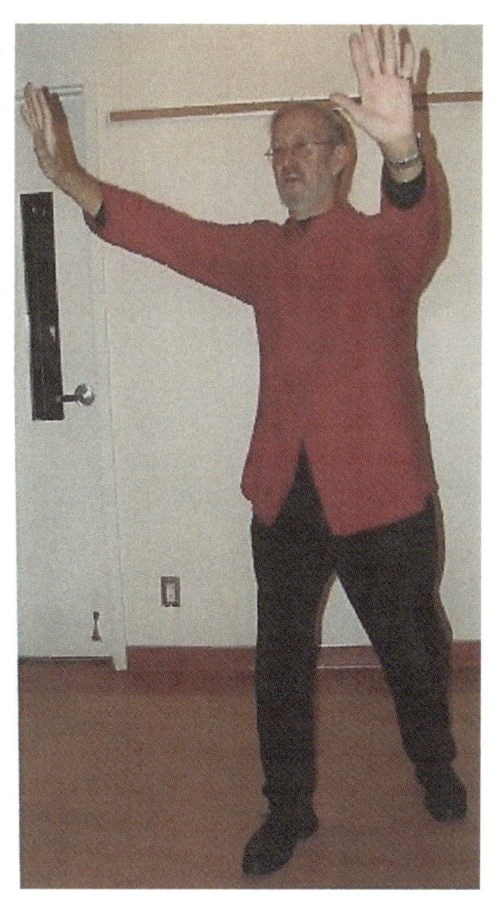

In the Story, you reach out to the struggling bird trapped in the net. Disentangle it, hold it gently in your hand and release it away from the net. We do it for as many birds as are trapped in the net. But remember, as I failed to do when trying to release a young blackbird from the net over a pen of young Trumpeter swans, that the birds may be very frightened and may peck you.

The Eagle Flies above the Valley.
Station 7

Tai Chi Movements 9. 10, 11
Fly with the Eagle, Wave Hands Like Clouds.

Another group of complex Tai Chi moves has also been made simpler for the Monkey Mountain story.

"Fly with the Eagle" begins a series of moves in Yang Tai Chi that include "Single Whip" and the beautiful moves called "Wave Hands like Clouds".

In the Monkey Mountain story the series begins with seeing the eagle flying over the valley and spreading your arms to "Fly with the Eagle". This move is based on an important way of increasing blood in the upper body taught in Ch Kung practices and in Dr Peter Kung Yang's traditional Tai Chi set which forms part of the Monkey Mountain story, later on down the mountain.

The next move in Yang Tai Chi is called "Snapping the Single Whip". This is a complex attack, hold or strike move. It is done fast and unusually aggressively for a Tai Chi move, and is more commonly learned in detail in harder styles of martial arts. I have been shown how it might be used but have never found a use for it in Push Hands. Throw one hand out like a whip and curve that hand down, like an eagle's beak.

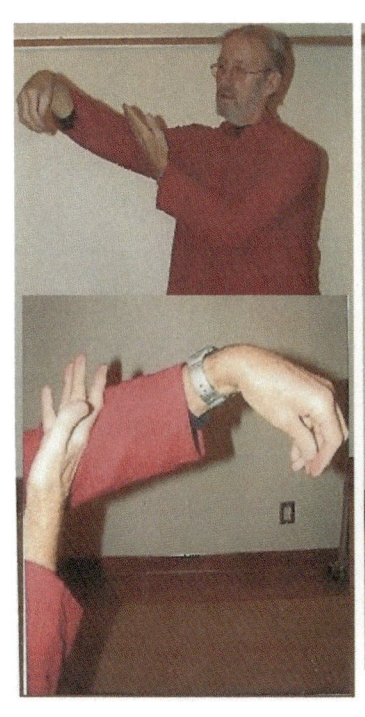

The curved hand can be a backhand fist, a curved hook around a neck, or a sharp weapon of nails and fingers into the base of the head. The other hand scoops up into the crook of the opposite elbow. Then it grips, perhaps the collar of a garment or the throat, and turns outward.

Single whip can also be described as "becoming an eagle". This is how this move is interpreted, simplified and made more gentle in the Monkey Mountain story. The hand becomes the head of the eagle when the hand in the "Single Whip " curves over to resemble the head and beak of an eagle. The other hand reaches up into the crook of the whip arm to mimic the folded wing of the eagle. Then, in the next move of the story, open your arms to begin the series of beautiful moves called "Wave Hands Like Clouds" in Yang Tai Chi and in the Monkey Mountain story.

Tai Chi Move 10
Wave Hands Like Clouds

In the Monkey Mountain Story this series of moves begins with the image and the movements of an eagle soaring over the mountains and the valleys. It turns into waving one's hands like clouds.

I learned this move under my first teacher, Master Moy Lin Shin. It was used to introduce and teach you the turning, twisting, and stretching your waist, your spine, your shoulders and each of your hands in Tai Chi.

These spiraling movements, to the right and to the left, were among the important things in the younger person's way of learning to do "Wave hands like clouds". The turning was also important in most of the 108 moves of Master Moy's Tai Chi. This was all part of this Master's special process to correct the emphasis on muscular strength rather than relaxation and chee energy that affected many in the westr. This was the approach to health through Tai Chi that he brought to North America and that he named Taoist Tai Chi.

North American bodies, Master Moy explained, are accustomed to tensing to use the muscles of the upper body. "You have big muscles but shortened ligaments for strength in the west", he would explain. "So I will teach you to stretch and turn your limbs, to loosen you up and use the twisting of the hips and of your back so that in time you will relax. Then you will use the natural strength of your spine and your legs and to let the "Chee" flow through your whole body from your toes to your finger tips".

I remember meeting a retired farmer, big framed and strong.But he had intense back pains from his constant work and lifting as a dairyman, now that he was retired. I showed him Master Moy's Tai Chi. I hope he is doing it and benefiting from it. Master Moy developed his ideas for Tai Chi so as to twist and stretch all parts of the body. "If you would have a thing shrink, you must first lengthen it", says the Tao Te Ching. "If you would have a thing become more gentle, you must first strengthen it," said Master Moy.

Our story continues. You, now and eagle, fly over to the roof of a temple.

Station 8
The Temple of the Buddhist Monks;

Yang Movements 11. 12.
The Eagle flies to the roof of the Temple. The Round Door opens. The Buddhist monks play Kung Fu

"**Single Whip and High Pat on the Horse**" are the Yang Tai Chi set moves that end the "Waving Hands like Clouds" and begin the visit to the monks of the Buddhist Temple to do Kung Fu exercises with them.

In the trip up Monkey Mountain the "waving hands like clouds" movements end when the player once again becomes the eagle. The eagle flies with spread wings over to the roof of a temple on the side of the mountain. The round door into the temple courtyard opens. Inside the monks are doing their daily kung fu exercises.

The eagle flying to the roof of the temple images from the Monkey Mountain story replace another striking move of the Yang style set that begins the kick series of Tai Chi moves. The "High Pat on the Horse" Yang Tai Chi move is more complicated and advanced than is needed for us doing the Monkey Mountain story Tai Chi set for health and recreation. "High Pat on the Horse" will be left to be learned later as part of a more advanced stage of Tai Chi.

In the Temple, the next set of movements will test your balance and your spirit with moves based on how Tai Chi and other martial arts use the legs and the fists for physical defense.

Movement 13.
Play Kung Fu with Monks. Kick with the Right Foot. Step Forward, Cross Your Hands and Kick with the Left Foot.
These are the first moves of the young monks as they practice and play their daily kung fu in the courtyard of the temple.

Kicks are a spectacular and athletic part of martial arts and of Tai Chi. They are used for self defence and attack. But they are also important ways to improve and test leg strength, balance and coordination. The so-called Tai Chi heel kick, with the heel forward and the toes up, is deceiving. It is quite different from the usual kick, such as that delivered in football with the foot and leg driving through in time with running forward. The so-called kick in Tai Chi is much more controlled.

How high one kicks or can kick depends on how strong and flexible your legs are. Because stability is more important than speed in doing Tai Chi moves, the leg kicks are first done slowly. It is wise to place chairs on either side of an older person, early in their playing the Monkey Mountain trip, before they try these kicks, just to be safe.

Step forward, cross your hands in front of the other knee. Lift the knee and straighten the leg. For a heel kick, keep the toe up. For a toe kick, also called a separation, point the toe. For the separation, swing the toe outward. In Northern China martial arts and Japanese Karate, the toe separations are done jumping and with the legs held high and moving fast. These are impressive but not always as strong as they look.

The test of a strong, stable Tai Chi kick would be to push open a heavy door in front of you with your foot and heel.

The crossed hands that precede the kick do two things. The crossed hand movement sets one's weight in the rear leg, ready for the strong forward push with the other leg as it kicks out. The crossed hands also protect low and with the lift, intercept any kicks thrown towards you, lifting the attacking leg and probably the kicker too.

The crossed hands rise up and separate as one kicks. One hand pushes in the same direction as the kick. Some players slap the kicking foot. The other hand stretches out to the side, to protect and help keep balance. The kick is completed when the kicking foot drops back down to the ground in front of you. You are ready to reach down, cross hands to kick again with the other foot. In the 108 move Tai Chi sets you step back, turn, face the rear and do other kicks right and left, behind you, to the four points around you. In the Monkey Mountain set all kicks are done to the front to make it easier to follow your leader.

Your leader will act as your "young monk" to show you how to kick and practice carefully. He or she should also make sure that early attempts are done with the back of a chair beside you for safety.

After one or two kicks the leader will step back and "box ears'. This is also called "strike ears with fists".

Move 14.
Strike Ears with Fists

Boxing somebody's ears looks amusing but is quite an aggressive move. If used accurately it is a downright dangerous double hand blow to the temples on the sides of the head. But as a Tai Chi exercise it has a wonderful full arm stretch and twist and an enjoyable spirit lifting crunch at the end. You use the first knuckle on each hand to deliver the boxing strike. You can hurt yourself doing it too energetically. It is done with one foot in front of the other, stepping forward or back. This move can seriously hurt someone's temples if aimed at them.

The move begins with the two hands in front of you, palms up at waste height,. Pull the hands back and out in a wide curve, twisting your hands down and out until the palms face out. Lift both hands up. The twisting is strong but controlled, especially with the shoulders relaxed. Stretch your hands out as far as possible on each side of you. Begin to lift the finger tips and close your fists. Your fists will rise shoulder high. Bring, or rather snap them together, the first knuckles facing each other. Be sure there is no head between them.

This move can also be done elegantly and smoothly. Sweep the hands out in a wide twist. Close the fists and bring them quickly up to within inches of each other. It works best with the shoulders relaxed. The curving twist of the hands and arms, completed by the rising fists is an impressive exercise.

Move 15.
Cross Hands and Do a final Kick with the Left Foot.

In the Yang short set, the player will complete a kick, then step forward, strike ears. Then, turning both feet on the heels, the player will turn completely around, step forward with the right foot, cross hands and kick to the rear with the left foot. Monkey Mountain story has eliminated this turn around to make it easier to follow a leader.

So, in front of the Temple courtyard for the Monkey Mountain story, we will step back and follow our leader and " strike ears with fists" to the front .Open your ear boxing fists and bring your hands down. Cross them. Raise your left knee and kick again. This can be done with the foot extended and usually results in a swinging sweep. This, in martial arts, would be called a separation with the extended foot.

The monks complete their exercises, the round temple door closes.

Station 9
Going Down the Road Below the Temple.

Movement 16.
Creep Low Like a Snake (Sweep snakes off the road) and **17. Rise Up Like a Golden Rooster** (Avoid stepping on other snakes)

"Creep Low like a Snake" is a Tai Chi move often used in sculptures as the signature movement of Tai Chi. It can be a move for the younger, the strong and flexible legged, or the ambitious.

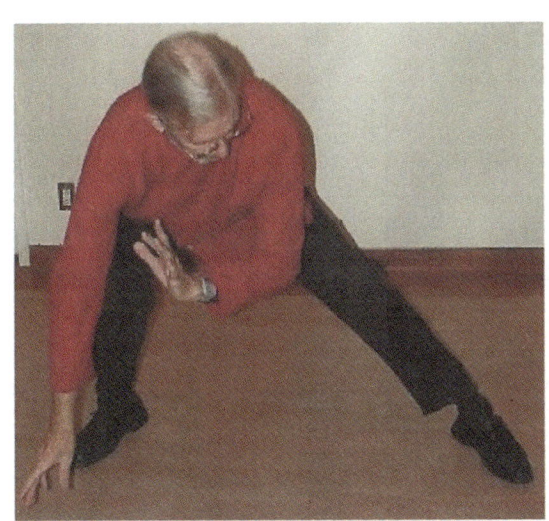

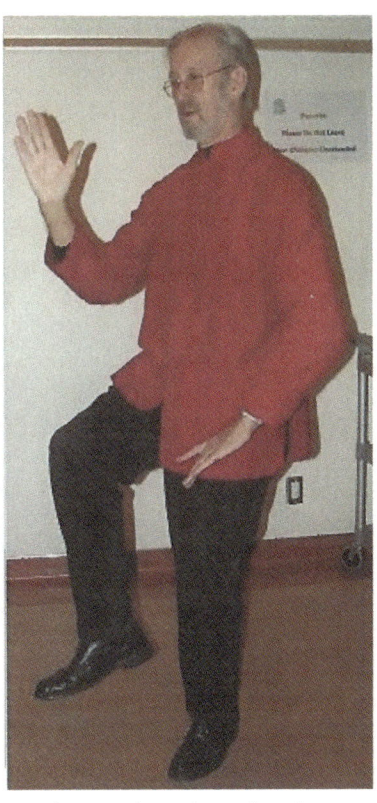

In this move one sits as low as one can on one side and stretches the other leg out to the side. How far out depends how low one can sit, how strong your legs are. One hand, curved over like an eagle or a snake's head, stretches out behind you. Then both hands sweep down "low like a snake". Your weight moves across from one leg to the other and the knee rises up as the hands rise to make the "Golden Rooster" form. Then you curve one hand, reach it out to the other side, sit low on this side and sweep both hands across "low like a snake, and stand up "Like a Golden Rooster" on the other side.

For many older native Chinese who squat down low to sit all their lives, this is not a difficult move, even for seniors. For North Americans and the rest of the world the chair has deprived us of opportunities to squat down. By middle age, the legs are so weak and the joints so stiff, that "Creeping Low Like a Snake" takes a long time, much practice and development to begin to perform it, or to do it at all.

For the Monkey Mountain trip, we begin reaching down to pick berries by the road. Then you can show the creeping down to throw a snake off the road, rise up to avoid stepping on it, and ask the trippers to try it. In time this becomes a good leg strengthening and flexing exercise. And you can always ask your senior Chinese to demonstrate. You will be impressed, if not amazed.

Station 10
The Village of the Weavers
Movements 17, 18.
Fair Ladies Throw Shuttles

Down the road, we hear singing, chatter and laughter. In the village square the ladies of the village have gathered as they do each fine day with their weaving looms.

"Throwing Shuttles" is a fine exercise for the waist and the muscles that turn the waist, the legs and the back. We join the ladies throwing shuttles. Your hands pick up the shuttle on one side of the loom. Step out and keeping the shuttle level by rotating you hands, throw it across the loom. Pick up the shuttle on the other side, step out and repeat the throw to the other side.

You begin to use the chee in your waist area as "a fair lady throwing shuttles", turning your stomach area, or your internals, as more advanced Tai Chi players call it, for each throw. You can end up throwing the shuttles with your abdomen. This is the beginning of doing internal Tai Chi.

"Throwing the Shuttles" like other Tai Chi moves is a throw as well a turn, a push and a stretch. It uses spirit, heart and yang chee energy to project the shuttles across the width of the looms.

The ladies stop for tea. We carry on our trip towards home now, in the Tai Chi set and the Monkey Mountain story. We head for the village dock beside the river.

Station 11
Taking the Fisherman's boat across the river.
Movement 19.
Reach for the Needle at the Bottom of the Ocean

Except for the bows of greeting which can be done before or after the set, there are few moves in Tai Chi that stretch the back. "Step up, Reach Down for the Needle at the Bottom of the Ocean" begins by stepping a half step forward. Now sit back. Raise the right hand high above your head, fingers pointing to the sky. Relax. Drop your chin and I like to explain the move, roll yourself up like a swiss roll cake as you plunge that hand down into the "sea".

The needle at the bottom of the ocean is an image from the famous Chinese legend about the priest, the monkey and his friends who brought the Buddha's teaching sutras back to China from India, a long time ago. The needle you reach down for is one of the legendary story's golden needles. Each golden needle turns into a fully armed monkey warrior when pulled up. Cross you hands down low and then roll your back up and lift your hands up to shoulder height. Now, open your hands apart like the opening of a fan.

Of course in the Monkey Mountain story we have changed this move. We go down from the village center, climb into a fisherman's boat for a trip over the river to our own village. I like to show the bow of the boat. Then I copy the fisherman rowing, the Chinese way, pushing forward on the oars not the Atlantic and Mediterranean pulling.

At the fisherman's suggestion, you raise your arm and turn it into a fishing rod. Throw out the line, you hand plunges down, sending your line to the bottom of the lake. Pulling the line in, you soon have caught a fine silver carp. They are big, as big as your hands can stretch apart. Like " Reaching for the Needle", your fishing is done by stepping forward with your left foot, sitting back down on the right leg, with the left leg forward to maintain balance, raise your right arm as the fishing rod. Throw out the line. Without leaning forward, lower the right hand straight down beside your thigh, the baited line goes down into the lake, like "reaching for the needle". Your right leg will take all your weight as the hand drops as far as you can. In Yang Tai Chi, your hands cross at the lowest point. You raise them up, crossed to shoulder height. In the Story, you hook a fine big fish, or just a minnow.

Move 20.
Yang Tai Chi's "Open the Fan to the Back"
In our Monkey Mountain story; How big was the fish you caught? Raise the sails of the boat. Show the breadth of the waters of the lake.

In Yang Tai Chi this move is done by turning and facing behind you, thus "Opening the Fan to the Back". We don't bother with the turning around in the Monkey Mountain story so we are still facing the front and our leader's back when we copying "Opening the Fan".

Zhu Gwang Ya, my second teacher, brought me the 24 Move Yang Set from China. "Opening the Fan" was his favorite Tai Chi move. He was the first to teach me a kind of Tai Chi that more closely follows the Tao's principles of never taking movement to an extreme. These principles began by emphasizing Tai Chi walking. For Yang Tai Chi that Gwang Ya brought from Southern China and now for the Monkey Mountain Story the way to walk is for the feet to be one third of a pace apart, about the width of standing normally, and to take each step straight forward as you move. This requires the turning of the foot before each next step forward.

These walking movements and the sweep of the hands ,"combing the wild horse's mane" in the early moves of this story and set, or the push forward as we climb up the mountain, or the ward off , block and push of "grasping the birds tail", are never full blocks and pushes. They are one point in a moving series of forms that link all the moves of Tai Chi, forward, sideways or backwards into a gentle but strong whole. This is one of the stages in learning Tai Chi. Whether just twenty four, 43, 65 or 108 moves, all parts of the Tai Chi set or a trip up Monkey Mountain become one continuous dance with patience and practice.   First you learn and learn to enjoy each new move of the Story and Tai Chi. Then as you make the sets part of your life you begin to learn more.

A move as interesting as "Open the Fan" makes this easier. Showing how big a fish you have caught is even easier, and just as pleasing.

This elegant move begins with the hands crossed at shoulder height in front of you, palms toward you. You open the fan by moving your hands apart, at the same time turning the palms out. Your fingers become the spines of a fan, opening out the fan in front of you.

In the Monkey Mountain story you show the length of the fish you just caught. Because this is move is good for the shoulders, and because Master Zhu liked it, we do it again, this time stretching the arms up high, rising and opening like the sails of the fishing boat. Then a third time, stretch the turning hands out at shoulder height like the waters you are about to cross.

We cross the river, here wide as a lake. Here the Monkey Mountain story takes a diversion into some moves from another Tai Chi story and set, Dr. Peter Yang's "Traditional Tai Chi Set".

Station 12
The Lotuses by The Landing

By the dock of our village we learn from the fisherman how lotus water lilies grow and how the energies of the sun and the earth display themselves. This was described in the Monkey Mountain story.

Station 13
The Island and Cave of the Dragon and Phoenix

These parts of the Monkey Mountain Story and set come from Dr. Peter Yang's "Old Traditional Set" story. Moves mimic and describe an angel that flies like a dragonfly across the the lake. There the Yang energy dragon roars out from his cave and the beautiful Ying energy Phoenix flies across the lake and are described by the fisherman. This can be one ending to the Story and its Tai Chi set.

Now we return to the moves of the usual ending of the Short Yang Tai Chi set. For these last few moves of the set we leave the fisherman's boat where he landed at the dock below our own village. We pick up our fish and the things we bought from the Village of the Weavers, we now walk up from the dock and meet the wood seller.

Station 14
The Old Wood Seller on the Dock

Move 21. Turn and Chop With Fist (The woodsman chops kindling)
Move 22. Parry, Deflect and Punch (The woodsman saws another piece of log)

To raise your spirits the last two moves of the set itself begin with a swinging chop with the back of the fist. This is followed by a step forward, a parry with the hand and a deflection like the one as the first move of "Grasping the Bird's Tail. But this time it is completed by a powerful punch with the clenched fist.

The Monkey Mountain story describes these moves as chopping kindling for the oven and then, when the old woodsman asks, picking up a saw and cutting off another length of log for the next person to chop into kindling, remembering that oriental saws, like those used by my wood carver friend Frank Mongeau on Vancouver Island, cut on the back stroke, rather than on the forward push like western saws. OK?

Move 23.
Apparent Close Up

When you complete the punch in the Yang Tai Ch set, cross your forearms and draw them in towards your chest, palms inward. This changes to a strong push outward from what was an "apparent" close up.

From this move, from Master Moy, I learned one of the strongest movements of Tai Chi, "the step up push". Coordinating your step up with the push out with your hands, you deliver your strongest and fastest possible push outward. It will be a surprise to the person in front of you. We usually had one or two people standing behind them to catch them.

This move does not fit well into the Monkey Mountain story and I don't usually show the half step push to beginners. So we proceed to the end of the set and the story.

Station 15
Return Home to the Cottage
Move 24.
Gather Up and the Conclusion of the story and the Tai Chi set

To end the story and the Yang set, you reach down to gather up the things you have acquired on the trip to Monkey Mountain, a blanket or scarf from the village of the fair lady weavers, your fish from the river and the kindling.

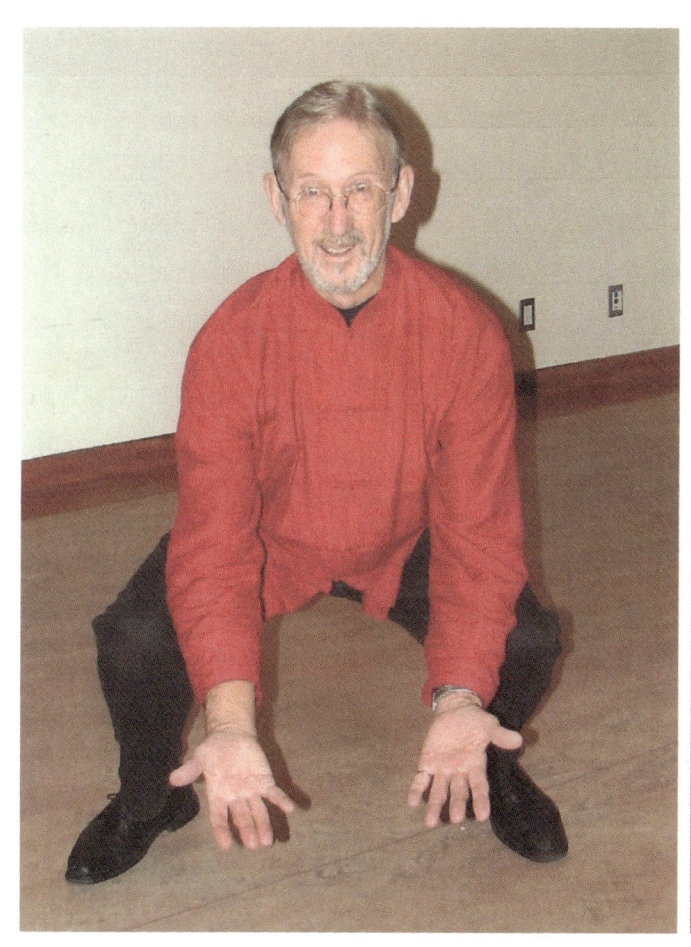

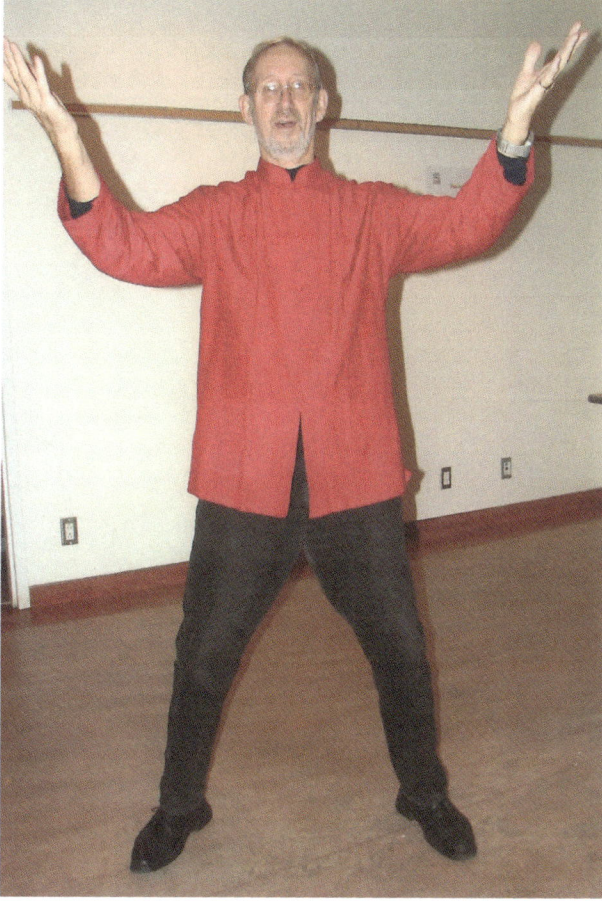

This is a last test of your legs to remind you of all the work, strengthening and flexing, that is needed to make them stronger and this move easier. Place the things down on the cottage kitchen table. You conclude your Tai Chi set and the Monkey Mountain story with your arms again rising and lowering like the sun. Your body has benefitted from the series of moves. Your mind has cleared as you concentrated on the sequence of the set. And your heart is uplifted by the charm of the Story and the art of Tai Chi.

Here is where you do the Tai Chi bows described in the Monkey Mountain Story.

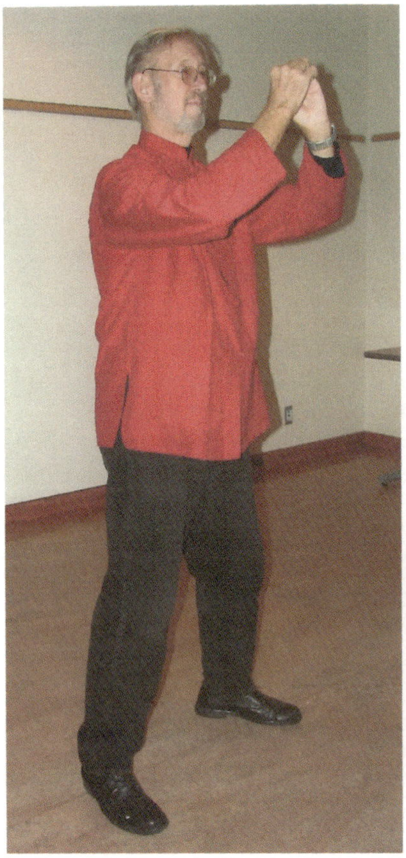

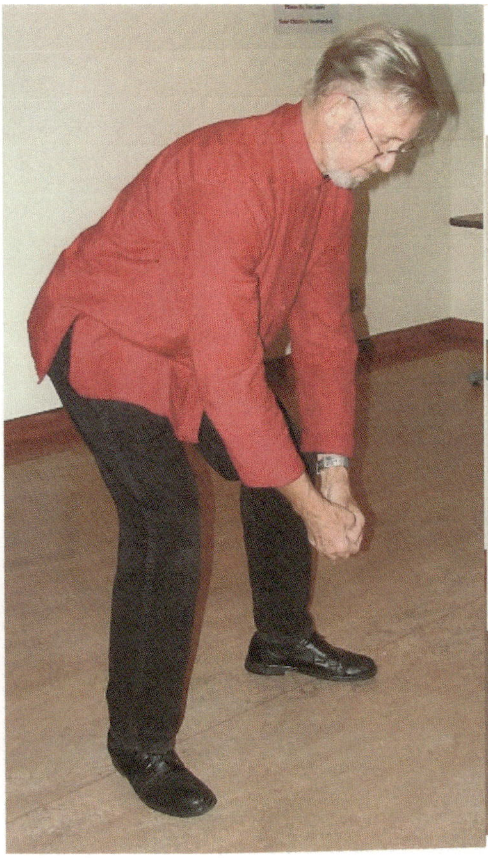

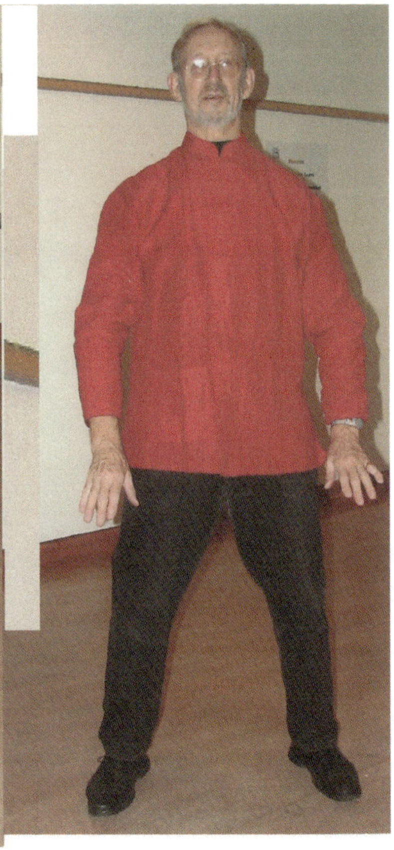

Chapter 5

The Animals in the Monkey Mountain Story

Genghis and Rascal with Michael White, 2006

Some animals play parts in the Monkey Mountain Story. These animals, are small stuffed realistic toys. They naturally joined in the playing of Monkey Mountain Tai Chi as the story developed. Now after many years they have become part of leading the Story in many places and situations. In nursing homes, they are small, familiar and comforting little fellow participants in the story, that sometimes go home with the players. In teaching classes, they add to the richness of the images and the imagination of the story and even add to more serious Tai Chi teaching.

Who are they?

First of all there are the monkeys, the namesake of the whole story and this Tai Chi. They began with a single little toy, whom we named Rascal. He was a beautifully and sturdily made little Leaf Monkey, No. HAN3648 in the catalogue of Portraits of Nature series made by Hansa Toy International Inc.

Next came the "Noisies". The original "Noisies" were humorous little toys called "Flingshot Flying Monkeys" made by Playmaker Toys of Kowloon and Hong Kong. They occasionally wake up sleepy wheelchair players. They also give a natural startling noise that adds to the heightened awareness for the important "Stepping Back and Repulsing Monkeys" Tai Chi moves. They add to the realism of the trip up the Mountain and the image of monkey challenged Lookout up there.

A number of Hansa Rascals were followed by many different monkeys from many different toy makers, mostly in the 15 to 25 cm size range but often with much longer tails. They all found places in the story and in the games and the humor surrounding the trips up Monkey Mountain, the warm-ups and learning the Tai Chi moves at the Stations up the mountain.

The next important member of the Monkey Mountain family was "Genghis" the Mongolian Pony. The first and several subsequent ponies have been TY Beanie Baby, ponies. Smaller ponies have tried to become part of the story but they do not have the necessary presence to lead in the difficult process of learning Tai Chi walking.

A visit to a Northern New York State Lake Environment exhibit provided soft and realistis toy fish for the lake in the Monkey Mountain landscape. Beautifully made juvenile sturgeons, trout and bass filled in for the silver carp and other species of western Chinese rivers and streams. Tellus provided bright little fish to add to the playful lake image needed for taking up the fisherman's fishing rod, throwing out the line, reeling in and measuring the size of your imaginery catch with Tai Chi's " Opening the Fan" movements.

Small bird toys came to the story in several ways. The Audubon Society's delightful Bird Song series have provided many smaller realistic, soft, colourful and songfull toys to be freed from the hunters' nets beside the roadway as we come down the mountain from the Monkey Lookout.

Eagle and Crane models did not come into the Day to Day trips up the Mountain. Either too large or too small, model toys of these members of the Monkey Mountain story's cast generally were too realistic, bizarre or frightening to easily join in the play.

Bells also became part of the story. Small jingle bells around Genghis' neck have served well. First they are the old hermit's bell on top of the mountain, summoning the monkeys away from the lookout to their prepared food, freeing us climbers from the attentions of the monkey band. Then in the village of the weavers, a bell signals tea break time for the hard working ladies and is time for us to head down to the dock for our boat ride home across the river.

The Tiger Cub and the little Panda cub joined the story because of the high quality of these toys' soft realism and their appropriate scale. It was found, that in addition to being pleasing and popular, they were able to be fitted into some useful Tai Chi teaching. Reaching back to pick up the little toy tiger cub or panda was an effective way to teach turning the attention, the hips and the balance in the important, "Climbing the Mountain" movements. Who three repetitions carry the story player through the farmers' gate and up across fields, up through wooded slopes and up to the Lookout in a series of movements in the story, particularly when the classical name for this Tai Chi movement is the enigmatic " Protect your knee and Carry a Tiger up the Mountain".

Together with the picture size banner of the Monkey Mountain, village and the valley itself, the animals of the Monkey Mountain story have become important teaching tools. They help the imagination. They are often familiar little friends in the important work of encouraging people, sometimes sceptical and busy, sometimes severely handicapped people, to exercise their bodies, their minds, their imaginations and their emotions, including their sense of humor. The Animals have become real parts of the Monkey Mountain Story and Monkey Mountain Tai Chi.

Annex 1

The 15 Stations along the Trip Up and Down Monkey Mountain.

The Stages in the Story

The Trip up Monkey Mountain can be divided into 15 different Stations. At each of these stations, one or often several Tai Chi movements from the Yang Tai Chi set or the "Old Traditional Set" are learned and performed. The Stations and the visual picture of where each of them fits into the story of the trip up the mountain. They are designed to help leaders, learners and players remember and visualize the movements and the sequences that connect them with each Station.

The 15 Stations

Station 1 of the Monkey Mountain Story; In the Morning, outside the back of the Cottage. The Sun rises.

Station 2, Monkey Mountain
The Ponies in the Field,

Station 3
The Bridge and the White Cranes.

Station 4
Climbing Monkey Mountain Ridge.
Three Steps.

Station 5
The Lookout and the Monkeys. The Hermit

Station 6
The Road Down the Back of the Mountain.
Free the Songbirds

Station 7
The Eagle Flies above the Valley.
Waves Hands Like Clouds

Station 8
The Temple of the Buddhist Monks;

Station 9
Going Down the Road Below the Temple.

Station 10
The Village of the Weavers

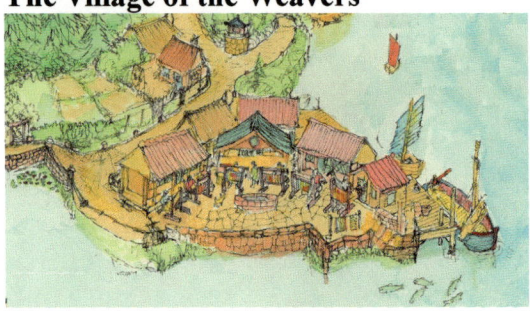

Station 11
Taking the Fisherman's boat across the river.

Station 12
The Water Lillies by The Landing

Station 13
The Island and Cave of the Dragon and Phoenix

Station 14
The Old Wood Seller on the Dock

Station 15
Return Home to the Cottage

Annex 2

Short Instructions and the Names of the Moves for doing Yang Style Tai Chi and other exercises

The 24 Moves of the Yang Short Form Tai Chi
(and the Monkey Mountain Story and Set Variations)

1. **The Sun Rises**
2. **Combing the Wild Horse's Mane; step to the left and to the right, comb the pony's mane each step, at least three times** (In the MM set; Saddle the pony, ride toward the Mountain, to the bridge)
3. **White Cranes Cool their Wings**
4. **Carry the Tiger up the Mountain; done to the left and the right, at least three times** (In the MM set; open the gate into the fields, through the rice paddies, through the trees, up to the Lookout)
5. **Step Up and Play The Fiddle**
6. **Step Back and Repulse Monkeys; done to the left and the right at least 2 times each side**(In the MM set; add The Hermit's Bell Rings)
7. **Grasp the Bird's Tail to the Left** (In the MM set; Free the Songbird from the Hunters' Net)
8. **Grasp the Bird's Tail to the Right** (In the MM set; Free the Songbirds. Lower the Net)
9. **Single Whip** (In the MM set; Your right hand becomes the Eagle's head, your hands then becomes its wings)
10. **Wave Hands Like Clouds: done at least three times to each side** (In the MM set; The eagle swoops down through the mists over the lake and up into the sky, left hand, then right hand. Then

wave hands like clouds)

11. **Single Whip,** 12. **High Pat on the Horse** (In the MM set; Eagle Flies to the roof of the Temple. Open the round Courtyard door, join the young monks' kungfu exercises)

13. **Cross Hands and Kick with the Right Foot** ((In the MM set; cross hands and kick with the right heel and and then cross hands, kick, point with the left foot).

14. **Strike Ears with Fists** (In the MM set; Step back and strike ears with fists)

15. **Turn to the rear, Cross Hands and Kick with the Left Foot** (The turn not done in MM set. Last kick. Cross Hands and Kick with the left Foot, the Temple Door closes)

16. **Creep Low Like a Snake; done to the left and the right** (In the MM set; Pick flowers and berries from the roadside. Sweep snakes off the road down the mountain)

17. **Rise Up Like a Golden Rooster; done to the left and the right** ((In the MM set; lift your foot to avoid any more snakes!)

18. **Fair Ladies Throw Shuttles** (In the MM set; Join the Singing and Laughing Ladies in the Village Square, weaving. Throw shuttles, left and right)

18. **Reach for the Needle at the Bottom of the Ocean** (In the MM set; Fishing and Crossing the Lake)

19. **Open the Fan to the Back** (In the MM set, done three times; How big is the Fish, Raise the Sails, skim across the water)

Different Endings for the Monkey Mountain Story

Here the moves from Dr. Peter Yang's Old Traditional set can be substituted for the visit to the woodsman. These moves will include taking the sunshine's energy down the stems of the lilly pads, the growing of new buds from the roots into lotus flowers. From here we follow the angel or the dragon fly to the cave of the dragon across the lake. We learn to roar like the dragon. Then we fly like the phoenix, settling and waving its colorful tail. Finally, to conclude Peter's short set we learn to use acupressure to the center of the palms of our hands, to bring energy to our heart cavity. These moves can be one ending for our trip up Monkey Mountain.

Or we can complete the 24 moves of the Short Yang Tai Chi set by continuing in the fisherman's boat to our own village dock. Here we will meet the woodsman and continue the story and the Yang Tai Chi set.

20. **Turn and Chop With Fist** (In the MM set; Meet the woodsman, chop kindling)
21. **Parry, Deflect and Punch** (In the MM set; For the woodsman, saw another length of log)
22. **Apparent Close Up** (In the MM set, this move is not done)

23. **Gather Up** (In the MM set; Your scarf or carpet, your fish, your kindling)

24. **Conclusion of Tai Chi** (In the MM set; Back at the Cottage, Place what you have gathered on the trip on the kitchen table, give bows of greeting to the Tai Chi tradition, to your teacher, to your friends and family, to yourself)

The Moves of Dr. Peter Kun Yang's Traditional Set

Most recently I have had the good fortune to be part of Dr. Peter Kun Yang's Sunday morning Tai Chi classes under the great red oak trees of Toronto's High Park. As well as teaching the short 24 Move Yang Tai Chi, Dr Yang teaches longer Tai Chi sets, and sets of Tai Chi sword each Sunday morning.

Then one day he introduced us to what he called "The Old Traditional Set" with its delightful images of lotuses, dragons, angels and phoenixes. I have asked Dr. Peter Yang and he has allowed me to add moves 6 to 11 of his Traditional set to become part of the trip up Monkey Mountain.

1. **The Sun Rises**
2. **Walk along the River, Under the Mountains**
3. **Waves roll at the Lake**
4. **Fly Like an Eagle.**
5. **Wave Hands like Clouds**
6. **Lotus Lillypads Take Sunshine to the Roots**
7. **Green Lotus Bud Rises from the Mud. The Lotusses Opens**
8. **Dragonfly flies like an Angel across the Lake**
9. **Yang Dragon Leaves its Cave**
10. **Ying Phoenix Flies to its Nest, Shakes its Coloured Tail**
11. **Gather Energy into the Heart**
12. **Conclusion of the "Old Traditional Tai Chi Set"**

The Monkey Mountain Story Warmup Set

The warm up set or series of moves is done before doing the Monkey Mountain story. It is done seated to relax the players before the trip up the mountain, except for the last moves.

1. The warm up begins with **The Sun Rises**. In your seats, raise and lower your hands in front of you, arms outstretched, up to the height of your shoulders. With your hands still up, relax your shoulders. Lower your hands and relax. Repeat two to four times.

2. **Hands Twisting.** Raise both hands in front of you. Lower your elbows.
With your hands held in front of you. Twist your hands. Turn your palms towards your face. Turn your palms away from you. Repeat, slowly at first and then faster. Learn the "Tiger's Mouth" form for your hands.

3. **Hands rotate** around each other. This exercise links your shoulder blades with your rotating hands. Begin by moving your shoulder blades. Then use your shoulders to rotate your hands around each other. You can add the second move of this exercise, Hands Twisting, by twisting your hands as you turn them around each other or by scooping your hands in towards you.

4. **Repulse Monkeys**, alternate pushing out with the left hand and the right hand. At the fullest extension of your arm, turn each hand palm up and draw it back. Turn your shoulders each time you push out.

5. **Turn from Side to Side.** To exercise the muscles around your hips, raise your hands in front of you. Move your weight from one side to the other. Repeat several times. You can also hold an imaginary

ball of energy between your hands and shift the ball and your weight from side to side, repeating the moves.

6. **Turn and greet**. Gently twist your whole spine, side to side the, to your left, to your right. You can repeat this sociably if you are in a group, greeting the people on each side of you, side to side.

7. **Leg Exercises.** Extend your legs, pull your toes and foot up. Push toes and foot forward, Repeat 5 to 10 times.
Then **rotate feet and ankles**.

8. **Neck exercise**. Lift your head and look up. Turn and look to one side. Look down. Look to the front of you.
   Repeat to the other side. Look up or look down to start. Look to the other side. Look down then to the front. Do this three times each day and you will avoid neck pain or stiffness.

9. **The Eye exercises**. This is an exercise to relax you and teach you to feel energy or the chee moving in your body. This will be the same chee that raised your arms as **the Sun Rises.** This is same chee that energises each action of our bodies.
For this exercise, you will lift your eyes up to the ceiling. Keep looking up but relax. You will feel the energy from your eyes moving back down to your internal center of energy in your abdomen when you relax. This center is called the Tan Tien in Chinese

   Now fill your eyes with energy again to look to one side. Again relax. Feel the movement of of the energy.

Then, drop your eyes down to the floor, and relax. Now look straight ahead, which is relaxed already. Next, you can focus on any object on the floor and you find that you will also use chee to focus. Relax again.

   Repeat this series of eye movements, relaxing after each. Your whole being will be relaxed, your mind cleared by your concentration.

   You will be ready to do some work that your legs will need for going up the mountain.

10. Stand Up and Sit Down. 5X. Essential Leg Strengthening Exercises

Place your feet as wide apart as your shoulders. Stand up from your chair slowly. Sit back down. Begin five times each day to strengthen your thigh muscles. Soon ten times will be easy.

Or add an alternate way to exercise the group of big muscles in your thighs. Stand up. Raise your hands like the Sun Rises exercise. Lower them. 2 or 3 times will warm you up. Raise your hands again. This time, lower your hands, at the same time bend your knees, as low as you are comfortable to go down. Raise your arms, straightening your knees and legs slowly, repeat three to five times until your thigh muscles burn. Do either or both of these exercises each day, 5 times to begin, then 10 or more.

A pleasing variation will help you to feel chee in your hands and a sense of lifting and flying. Raise your hands first, then raise your knees, straightening your legs. Repeat.

These exercise will take about 5 minutes. You can do them at home or with your group. You are now ready to do Monkey Mountain story Tai Chi Set, standing or sitting.

Exercise 4 a. Learn and Use "The Tiger's Mouth Form" for your hands in Tai Chi moves:

When repulsing Monkeys and for most of the movements in Tai Chi, your hands are held in the form called the **"mouth of a tiger"**. With this form for your hands, you will learn to hold each hand in a way that is at the same time strong and gentle, natural and relaxed. Your fingers and thumb of each of your hands will be open, relaxed and naturally strong.

To put your hands in the "mouth of the tiger " form for the first few times, grab one wrist tight with your other hand. Then open that hand to remove the wrist. Your fingers take the form of a tiger's mouth. Grab the other wrist to make the "tiger's mouth" form with your other hand.

Each of your hands is the mouth of the tiger is strong, full of teeth. But then, remember that the tigress can reach down, pick up her kitten in that great fanged mouth without hurting a hair on its small head. This is the gentle, relaxed, image of the hands of "Tiger Mouth" form used in Tai Chi.

As you push your hands forward, repulsing monkeys or climbing "up the mountain", each hand becomes as strong as the mountain itself as you move forward. But the hands move as slowly and gently as a tiger mother's mouth.

Standing Warmup Exercises

A Safety Tip for problems of balance in exercise 9, as you work to improve your balance and strengthen your legs with doing Tai Chi or the Monkey Mountain story, place chairs on each side, in front of or on either side of you, faced outwards. They will give support and confidence.

For exercises, 2 to 7, I have to thank my first teacher, Master Moy Lin Shin who called these the "Jong" exercises.

The Five Chee Kung Animals

There is an exercise which is based on how your internal energies, called ying and yang chee in Chinese, work on different organs and parts of your body. The Five Animals are part of the long time Chinese practice called "Chee or Chi Kung", translated as "Work with, or on Chee". There are close relationships between the study and practice of Chee Kung and learning and practicing Tai Chi. Many of the moves of Tai Chi have have been designed to work with Chee Kung.

1. Roar Like A Tiger; an exercise to concentrate chee, energy in order to strengthen the diaphragm and the Lungs

2. Moan Like A Bear ; for bringing Chee energy to the Liver

3. Stretch Up Like A Startled Deer; for the Kidneys

4. Float on the Wind Like an Eagle; lifting the arms brings chee energy for the Heart

5. The Monkey Seeks Its Food; clean you teeth with your tongue, swallow the saliva, enjoy eating even an imaginary meal, for the Digestive System

Annex 3

Where is Monkey Mountain?

Monkey Mountain in the story is a "Mountain of the Imagination". It could be anywhere.

Annex 4

References

1. D.C. Lau "Tao Te Ching" Penguin Books, 1963

2. D.C. Lau "Lao Tzu – Tao Te Ching" Alfred A. Knopf, 1994

3. Douglas Wile "Lost Tai Chi Classics from the Late Ching Dynasty, 1996

4. Manley P. Hall "The White Bird of Tao" 2nd Edition, The Philosophical Research Society, 1964

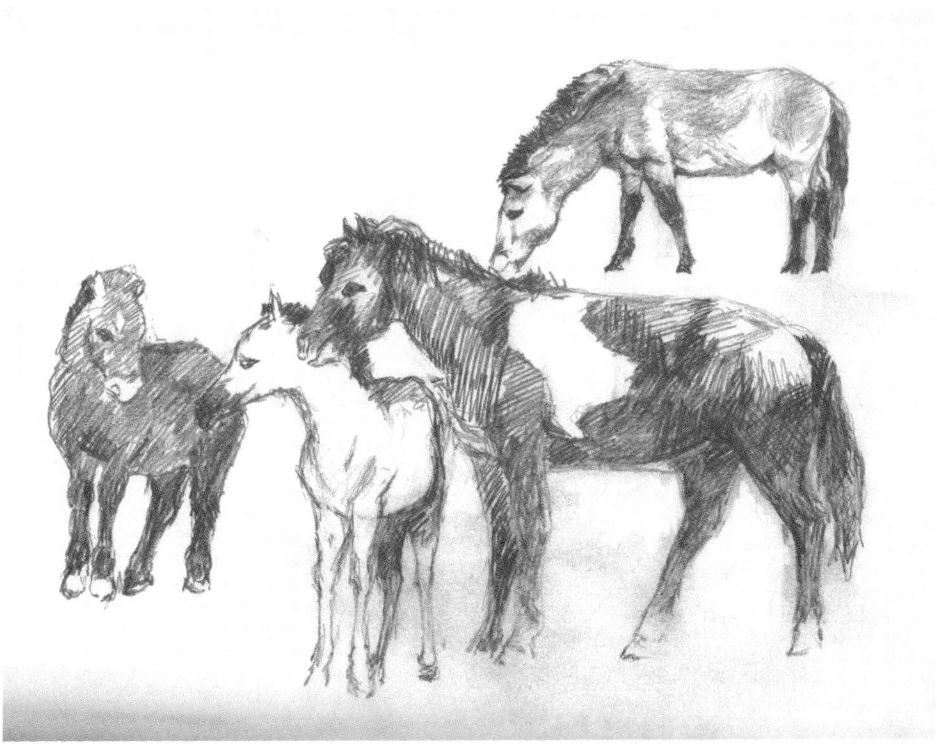

CPSIA information can be obtained
at www.ICGtesting.com
Printed in the USA
LVIC050537230513
334881LV00004B